Serve God with Gladness

A Manual for Servers

Children's Edition

David Philippart

LTP

LITURGY
TRAINING
PUBLICATIONS

For my parents,

Jane and Phil,

who not only encouraged me

to serve God with gladness

at Our Lady Gate of Heaven parish in Detroit

but even drove me to 6:30 AM Mass all week:

my love and gratitude.

Make a joyful noise to the LORD, all the earth.
   Worship the LORD with gladness;
   Come into his presence with singing.

Know that the LORD is God.
   It is he that made us, and we are his;
   we are his people, and the sheep of his pasture.

Enter his gates with thanksgiving,
   and his courts with praise.
   Give thanks to him, bless his name.

For the LORD is good;
   his steadfast love endures forever,
   and his faithfulness to all generations.

Psalm 100

Peter Spivak, who as a kid served God with gladness at St. James parish in Gadsden, Alabama, did the cover illustration and the illustrations on pages 3, 18, 48, 50, 55, 69, 72, 73, 75, 86, 88, 91 and 93, as well as the small icons used throughout the book. Photos on pages 22 and 29 are by Eileen Crowley-Horak. The photo on page 20 is © copyright James F. Housel. Photos on pages 7, 37 and 81 are by Antonio Pérez. Photos on pages 25, 44, 85 and 90 are © copyright Bill Wittman.

This book was edited by Martin Connell, who served God with gladness at Our Lady of Fatima parish in Secane, Pennsylvania. Audrey Novak Riley was the production editor, with assistance from Theresa Houston. It was designed by M. Urgo. Jim Mellody-Pizzato, who served God with gladness at Holy Ghost parish in South Holland, Illinois, set the type in Palatino and Smile. *Serve God with Gladness* was printed in the United States of America.

ISBN 978-1-56854-151-8

SERVER

15 14 13 12 11   9 8 7 6 5

Welcome!

Welcome to *Serve God with Gladness!* Maybe you have been serving Mass for a long time. Maybe you are just beginning to serve or just beginning to learn how to serve. Welcome!

My name is David. I wrote this book to help you serve better — by knowing what to do and why we do it. But this book cannot teach you by itself. Your parish leaders will show you how to serve in your parish. It is very important to listen to your leaders and follow their instructions. And the most important thing is PRACTICE!

How do you learn to play baseball? PRACTICE! How do you learn to play the violin? Or the kazoo? Or even the CD player? PRACTICE! How do you learn to dance? PRACTICE! Almost everything in life worth doing is worth practicing. So when your leaders schedule practice for you each week, don't miss it! It might seem boring — doing the same things over and over and over again in the empty church. But when it comes to your first Sunday, or the first Sunday when a new way of serving begins, you'll sure be happy about it. The crowds of people won't frighten you. And even if you think you are forgetting with your brain, your body will remember where to go and what to do.

Serving the holy people while we do our holy actions in the church is a way of growing closer to God. We cannot see God. But when we do something for the people that we do see, we do those things for God. Jesus promised that he would be with us when we gather. When we join in the liturgy, we remember Jesus and

> The most important thing is PRACTICE!
>
> How do you learn to play baseball? PRACTICE!

> How do you learn to dance? PRACTICE!

> How do you learn to play the violin? Or the kazoo? Or even the CD player? PRACTICE!

> Almost everything in life worth doing is worth practicing.

> When we serve God in church,
> we learn
> how to serve God
> outside of church:
> by helping
> people who are in need,
> by taking care of each other
> and the earth that we live on,
> by loving people
> that no one else loves.
> That's how
> we really serve God.

give thanks and praise for all the good things that God does for us. And God is mighty pleased.

Serving in the church is a special privilege. It allows us to be close to the altar, to carry the cross, to carry the light of Christ, to wear the robe of baptism, to hold the book of the prayers —and to swing the thing that makes the smoke (the thurible)! How wonderful this is!

This book can help you be a great server. Read it. Do the exercises. Keep it in a safe place. Read it over again.

This book can help you learn all about what we do in church. It has many strange and new words. Some are printed in **bold.** This means they are defined either in the glossary at the back of the book or on the same page. You can look them up and learn what they mean.

When I was in fourth grade, I really wanted to be a server. But in my parish, you had to be in fifth grade to serve. I could hardly wait. The next year I went to practice every Wednesday after school for half the year. Then I was scheduled to serve 6:30 AM Mass in the morning all week: Monday through Friday. It was hard to get up. But it was worth it. Serving Mass every day helped me learn how to serve. And after Mass, the woman who played the organ used to take the servers out for doughnuts! And once a year, the priests took us to the amusement park.

The first time I was scheduled to serve on Sunday, I was nervous! I made a few little mistakes, but everything went OK. The best advice I can give you is this: When you make a mistake, stop. Take a deep breath. Think: "What should I do?" Do it. Act like nothing is wrong. Then no one but you will know you made a mistake!

I loved serving in the church. And even now that I am grown up, sometimes I still do. Serving isn't just for kids! I hope that you will love to serve, too. I pray that you will learn to love the rites of our holy faith and serve the church with joy and with reverence (see page 7). And I hope that when we serve God in church, we learn how to serve God outside of church: by helping people who are in need, by taking care of each other and the earth that we live on, by loving people that no one else loves. That's how we really serve God.

Are you ready? Let's go!

David Philippart

Serving in the Assembly

One Body

The apostle Paul said that the church is like our own bodies. Our bodies each have many parts. We have eyes to see and ears to hear. We have mouths to speak and noses to smell. We have legs to walk, knees to bend, arms to reach, hands to hold. We have brains to think and hearts to love.

The church is Christ's body, made up of many parts. Christ is the head and we are the members. Christ calls together all the members of his body. Christ speaks to us in the scriptures. Christ invites us to pray, and we offer up our thanks and praise "through him, and with him, and in him." Christ lives in us when we share holy communion. And Christ sends us out of Mass to love and serve God by loving and serving other people.

The Mass is something that the whole body of Christ does — head and members together. It is not a play, where some people are actors and most people quietly watch. We do some things all together: like sitting, standing, bowing, singing, walking in procession. And different parts of the body do different things so that the whole body can celebrate. One person reads while all listen. Some people play musical instruments while all sing. Everybody prays quietly, then one person speaks for all. All of these things are done so that the whole body of Christ can give God thanks and praise.

Would you be able to run a race if your body was just a big eye? Would you be able to think if your body was just a big leg? All the different and wonderful parts of your body help you to be you. They help you to do different things.

It is like this with Christ's body, the church. The church has different parts — we call these **ministries.** Ministers do

CHRIST IS THE Head and we aRe the members of this BODY

different jobs to help the whole body of Christ worship God.

Many Parts

Christ is the head of the church and the first minister of the liturgy. When the church gathers for worship, we call the people, the body of Christ, the **assembly** or the **congregation.** These names mean that the baptized people (and the ones who want to be baptized) have come together in one place, have been called by God to gather in one place, to hear the word and share the holy meal.

The **sacristan** is the person who sets things up before liturgy and cares for the things that we use to worship God together. The sacristan works in the sacristy. Other people help, too: people who clean and who decorate the church's house, people who bake the bread for the eucharist, people who wash and iron the linens and vestments, people who train the ministers and make the schedules.

Ushers help the assembly gather together. They welcome strangers and visitors and help everyone find a place and be at home in the house of the church. They may pass out hymn books or song sheets. They collect the money and sometimes other gifts for the church and for the poor. They help make our processions orderly and joyful. They give people bulletins to take home.

Leading the assembly is the **presider.** The chief presider is the bishop. Since the bishop cannot be with all the churches at the same time, **priests** are chosen and ordained to lead the assembly in the liturgy. They lead the assembly in worship because they serve the church in other ways throughout the week.

The **deacon** sometimes helps the presider by preparing the gifts of bread and wine or holding the chalice. And the deacon leads us in worship by reading the gospel story, preaching the homily or leading the prayers of the faithful. Like a bishop, like a priest, the deacon is ordained, chosen by God to serve the church.

The **cantor** helps us all to sing. Sometimes the cantor sings alone so that we may all listen and then join in the singing. The **choir** is a group of singers who also lead the assembly in song. They make the song of the assembly beautiful by singing high and low, adding "parts" to the song. Other **music ministers** play instruments like the organ, the piano or the guitar.

Reading out loud (proclaiming) the first and second readings from the Bible are the **lectors.** The lectors also carry the book of the readings in procession. Like the prophets whose words they read, like Jesus, the lectors speak God's word.

The **communion ministers** share the body and blood of Christ with all the baptized. Some of them share the bread that is Christ's body. Some of them share the cup that holds the wine that is Christ's blood.

And helping to set things up and to put things away, carrying cross and candles and vessels of smoking incense, holding the book of the prayers, leading processions, assisting at the Lord's table with water and with wine are the servers — you!

On a baseball team, the players have different names that tell what they do: The pitcher throws the ball. The shortstop guards the space between

Find out the names of the people who serve your parish. Take this book to church next Sunday, and after Mass, ask one or two people who serve in the different ministries. You can write their names or have them sign your book. Make sure you tell them your name. Tell them that you are training to be a server.

The body of Christ at

Holy Cross

(write the name of your parish)

has many parts. Some I know, most I don't know. But we are all members of the body of Christ.

Some of the members of the assembly are:

Liam Gilligan, Lisa Valenzuela,

Some of the ushers' names are:

Rudy Quijauce
Kin Lazier/Sr
Kin Lazier/Jr

The bishop's name is:

Bishop Grasia

The priests' names are:

Father Joe
Father Jerry

The deacons' names are:

Deacon Hugo Patiño

One of the cantors is:

Victoria Perri

Some of the people in the choir are:

The director of music is:

Sister Barbra

Some of the lectors are:

Sister Barbra

Some of the communion ministers are:

Virginia Quijauce
Anne-Marie Mockus

Some of the other servers' names are:

Whittaker Miller,
Lexi Butler

The sacristan's name is:

The leader of the servers is:

Sister Barbra

Together we are the body of Christ!

To be a good server, do these good things:

At home:

1. Know when you are scheduled to serve. Mark it on a calendar. Hang the servers' schedule on your closet door or on the refrigerator. Tell your mom or dad. If you cannot serve when you are assigned, you will have to make sure that someone else will take your place. Tell your leader.
2. Before leaving home, wash your hands and face. Comb your hair. Brush your teeth. Wear good clothes. (Remember that you will put on a vestment over your clothes, so don't choose heavy clothes!) Wear your best shoes.
3. Say the prayer in the front of this book before you leave the house.

Preparing:

4. Come to church early, at least 20 minutes before Mass begins.
5. Put on your vestment. Make sure that it's not too long, not too short. Look in the mirror to make sure it's on right.
6. If your parish has an attendance sheet, sign it.
7. Help the sacristan or other ministers set up for the celebration. Put everything in its proper place. Set up quickly and quietly.
8. Carry things carefully, with both hands. Imagine that you're carrying eggs.
9. Bow when you pass by the altar. If you pass by the tabernacle, genuflect. But not if you are carrying something.
10. Use the bathroom before the celebration begins. Never leave during the liturgy unless it's an emergency.
11. When all the servers have arrived and everything is ready, decide which server is going to take which part (see page 33).

12. Relax and take some deep breaths before the celebration begins. Be calm.

Celebrating:

13. When you are not holding or carrying something, fold your hands.
14. Don't bow if you are carrying the cross, a candle or the book. If you pass by the altar while carrying or holding these things, stop and face the altar. Pause for a moment and look at the altar, but don't bow.
15. Carry things carefully, with both hands. Imagine that you're carrying eggs.
16. If you make a mistake or forget something, stay calm. Think before you act.
17. Walk and move slowly, but not too slow. Sit, stand and kneel straight and tall. Don't be stuffy, but on the other hand, don't be sloppy.
18. Don't whisper to the other servers. Don't walk around when it isn't necessary. Don't fiddle with things when you are in your seat — especially during the readings and homily.
19. Sing when the assembly sings, listen when the assembly listens, speak when the assembly speaks.

Cleaning up:

20. Wait until most of the people have left before going back to the altar.
21. Carry things carefully, with both hands. Imagine that you're carrying eggs.
22. Bow when you pass by the altar. If you pass by the tabernacle, genuflect. But not if you are carrying something.
23. Put things back in their proper places.
24. Hang up your vestment.
25. If you're the last one out of the sacristy, turn off the lights.

second and third base. The members of a symphony also have names: conductor, first violinist, kettle drummer. Here are some names for servers.

The server who carries the cross is called the **crossbearer,** or **crucifer.** The server who takes care of the bowl of burning incense is called the **thurifer,** because the incense bowl is called a thurible. Other servers don't have a specific name. Later, we'll make up some names for them! But these names aren't too important. They just help us practice how to serve. They help us make sure that each server knows what to do when.

A good server knows what to do and how to do it right. But there is more to being a good server than that. A good server is *reverent* and *responsible.*

What does it mean to be reverent? Does it mean to show reverence to God, to God's holy people? To treat the church building and all that is in it with respect?

Maybe it is easier to say what reverence is *not*. Reverence is not acting sad or silly, stuffy or stupid. Reverence is not pretending to be someone other than you, not pretending to be an adult when you are a kid. Reverence is not being a teacher's

To be reverent we have to use our minds, our hearts and our bodies.

To be reverent means to stand in wonder before something that is beautiful and great and important and holy.

pet. To be reverent doesn't mean that you have to act like a nerd.

Have you ever stared at the stars in the sky for so long that you stop seeing the stars and you start to daydream?

Or maybe you've sat still for a long time looking at a little baby. You watch the little one scrunch up its face and kick its feet and wave its arms and blow spit bubbles and make funny noises. And deep inside you feel love for this little baby. And maybe you wonder what it's thinking. And maybe you want to pick up the baby and hold it.

Have you ever picked up a seashell or a dried-up, empty cocoon, stared at it and said "Cool!"?

If you've ever done these things, felt this way, then you've been reverent. To be reverent means to stand in wonder before something that is beautiful and great and important and holy. To be reverent means to feel love and show respect for someone who is beautiful and great and important and holy. To be reverent we have to use our minds, our hearts and our bodies.

We use our minds to think about how beautiful and great and important and holy God is. We use our hearts to feel love for God and for the people of God. We use our bodies both to show our love and to help us love more, to be reverent.

How do we practice being reverent? First, use your mind. Remember that God is great and good. Remember that when the baptized people gather

> Underneath every seashell, in the twinkle of every baby's eyes, in the stories of every grandma and the silly jokes of every dad, God is waiting for us.

together, God is there. Second, use your heart. Pay attention to what you are doing. Third, use your body. Wash up. Comb your hair. Dress in your good clothes. Wear your best shoes. Walk slowly. Stand up tall. Sit up straight. Fold your hands when you are not carrying something. Carry things carefully. Bow smoothly.

And not only that. Listen when the scriptures are being read. Sing when the assembly sings. That's part of being reverent, too.

To be a good hockey player, to learn how to dance well, to skip rope with fancy tricks or jump curbs on a skateboard, you have to practice. Being reverent takes practice, too. Sometimes we forget. Sometimes we get the giggles. That's OK. The important thing is that we grow more and more reverent as time goes on.

Then we will never be bored. When we are good at being reverent, we know that the world is exciting because God is exciting. And underneath every seashell, in the twinkle of every baby's eyes, in the stories of every grandma and the silly jokes of every dad, God is waiting for us.

Be Responsible!

A good server is not only reverent. A good server is also responsible. Being responsible means:

- You come to practice and learn how to serve.
- You know when you are scheduled to serve.
- You come when you are scheduled.
- You find a sub when you cannot come.
- You come on time: 20 minutes before Mass begins.
- You come ready to serve God with gladness.
- You know what to do and ask when you don't.
- You help the other servers do a good job.

- You read this book over again after you've served for a while to brush up on what you know and to practice getting better at serving.

Being reverent and responsible is not boring or too hard. It's fun to do and it gets easier with practice! Will you try it? If so, sign your pledge to be reverent and responsible!

If you promise to try your best to be reverent and responsible, then you are ready to learn more about the Mass in the next chapter.

I Will Serve God with Gladness

With God's help, I

Katie Gilligan

(print your name here)

promise to be a reverent and responsible server at

Holy Cross

(print the name of your parish here)

I promise to come to practice, know when I'm scheduled to serve, come when I'm scheduled (or find a substitute) and come early. I will come prepared.

I promise to pay attention to the Mass, sing the songs, say the prayers and join in whatever the assembly does.

I promise to know my duties as a server and do them the best I can. I will ask questions when I don't know something.

I promise to treat the people of the church, the house of the church and all the things in it with love and respect.

I want to serve God with gladness!

Katie Gilligan

(sign your name here)

Fr. Terry Maher

(pastor's signature)

(signature of the leader of the servers)

Worshiping God Together

We are baptized. We belong to God. We belong to the community of God's people, the church. God calls us together: To be the church. To hear the word. To pray for others. To be born again in baptism's bath. To be fed with the bread of life and to drink the cup of salvation.

We do what Jesus told us to do: We gather together, listen to God's word, offer thanks and praise over the bread and the cup, and share the body and blood of Christ. We do this to remember Jesus, to love him and each other more. We do this *with* Jesus Christ.

Christ is with us in the assembly of the church. Christ is with us in the bishop, the priest and the deacon. Christ is with us in the word of God. Christ is with us in the bread and the wine after we give thanks and praise over them.

Sunday at My House

What are your favorite things to do on Sunday? Write or draw them in this box.

We gather together on Sunday, the day of the Lord. We sometimes have Mass on Saturday afternoon, too. Saturday afternoon is the time when we just can't wait for it to be Sunday!

Sunday is the first day, when God began creating the heavens and the earth, separating light from darkness. Sunday is the day that Christ Jesus rose from the dead, bringing us new life. Sunday is the day that the risen Christ appeared to the disciples and said "Peace!" Sunday is the day that the Holy Spirit came like wind and like fire. Sunday is the first day that the apostles were not afraid to tell everyone about Jesus. Sunday is the day for baptism. Sunday is the day for eucharist. Sunday is the day for the church.

We all come together on Sunday. We don't go to regular school. We don't go to work or we go at a different time. We join with our family and friends and even people that we don't know. All the baptized people and all the people who want to be baptized gather together.

We sing together. The whole assembly lifts up one loud voice. We have a parade called a **procession.** The cross is carried in and set up. We trace the sign of that cross on our bodies.

Sometimes we are sprinkled with holy water from the baptismal font. Other times we call out, "Lord, have mercy!" Sometimes we sing the song that the angels sang when Jesus was born: "Glory to God in the highest, / and on earth peace to people of good will."

Then we pray.

After we say "Amen!" to the prayer that the priest says aloud, we are ready to listen to God's word. We listen carefully. We listen carefully together.

We hear about what God has done. Then we sit quietly for a few minutes to think about it. We keep silence together: God speaks to us in the word and in the silence.

We sing a **psalm.** The cantor sings a verse and then we all sing it together. The cantor sings other verses and we repeat our part. God speaks to us in the singing.

We hear some advice about how to live good lives. Then we sit quietly again for a few minutes. We think about the advice. We keep silence together: God speaks to us in the word and in the silence.

Music starts and we jump to our feet, singing "Alleluia!" (Except in Lent — then we sing something else!) We know that now we will hear the gospel, the words and deeds of Jesus. We jump to our feet because we love the good news of Jesus. We stand at attention to listen with our hearts as well as our ears and minds. We trace the cross on our forehead, so that we may understand. We trace the cross on our lips, so that we may speak the gospel to others. We trace the cross on our hearts, so that we may love more and live by what Jesus says. We listen very carefully: God speaks to us in the gospel.

Then we sit for the **homily.** The priest, the deacon or another preacher helps us understand God's word. We listen very carefully.

At Mass, we listen to many Bible stories over the year. What's your favorite Bible story? Write or draw it in this box.

We Ask God's Help

After the homily, we say what we believe. The prayer is called the **creed.** Then we ask God for help. We pray for the church. We pray for the whole world. We pray for the sick, the suffering, the dying and the dead. The deacon or cantor or reader sings or says, "Let us pray to the Lord!" and we reply "Lord, hear our prayer!" "Lord, have mercy!" or some other petition.

We Prepare the Lord's Table

Gifts of money and sometimes other things are collected for the poor and for the church. The altar, the table of the Lord, is prepared. We bring bread and wine to the altar.

What prayers of asking for God's help do you want to pray?
Write some here:

....

....

....

....

....

....

....

....

....

Who are some people that need God's help? Write their names here:

....

....

....

We Give Thanks and Praise

"Lift up your hearts." the priest says. "We lift them up to the Lord." we all respond. This is how our great prayer of thanks begins. This is what we have come here for! To give God thanks and praise! For the sun and the moon. For the earth and the sky. For animals and for plants. For our family and friends. For our thoughts and our feelings. For our bodies and our minds. For life and for love and for Jesus. Especially for Jesus.

This is a long prayer. We must listen carefully to the words that the priest says. We must pray them in our hearts. We must sing our parts. We must stand up tall and kneel up tall as we give God thanks and praise.

Here are some things to know about the long prayer.

First, we tell God why we are giving thanks. Then we sing the Holy, Holy. This is the song that the angels sing to God in heaven. This is the song that the people sang to Jesus when he went to Jerusalem before he died and rose from the dead.

Next, we ask the Holy Spirit to come down on us and on our gifts. We remember that Jesus took bread and said, "This is my body." We remember that he took a cup of wine and said, "This is the chalice of my blood . . . Do this in

Write or draw one thing for which you want to say THANKS A LOT to God:

memory of me." He did and said these things on the night before he died.

Then we sing these words:
We proclaim your Death, O Lord, and profess your Resurrection until you come again.
or
When we eat this Bread and drink this Cup,
we proclaim your Death, O Lord, until you come again.
or
Save us, Savior of the world, for by your Cross and Resurrection you have set us free.

This song comes from our hearts. This song shows that we believe in all that Jesus has done for us.

Then we pray for the church, for the pope and for the bishop. We pray for the dead. We pray that one day we will all be together in heaven with Mary and all the saints.

To finish this great prayer, we sing the Great Amen. We sing this holy word to show that we believe in all that the priest has said, in all that we have prayed. We sing this holy word to show our joy for all that God gives us, especially the gift of the body and blood of Christ.

We give to God bread and wine. God gives to us the body and the blood of Christ. It still looks and feels and tastes and smells like bread, but it is the body of Christ. It still looks and feels and tastes and smells like wine, but it is the blood of Christ. How wonderful this is!

To prepare to share what Christ gives us, we say the prayer that Christ taught us: "Our Father . . ." Then we share a sign of peace with each other — a handshake or a hug. This helps us love and forgive each other more. This makes us ready to share in the holy supper, the bread of life and the cup of salvation.

We sing together, and the baptized people come to the table of the Lord to share communion. Each one is told, "The body of Christ" and then, "The blood of Christ." Each one answers, "Amen!"

The body and blood of Christ. That is another name for us. The church is Christ's body, Christ's blood. Each one of us is called "Christian" because we have been bathed in baptism and fed at the Lord's table. Just as the bread and the wine were changed, so we are changed. We live no longer just for ourselves. We now live to love and help others.

We Go in Peace
to Love and Serve

A few announcements may be made. Then the priest gives the final blessing. We go out. We go back home. We go to love each other more. We go to make peace with our enemies. We go to help the poor. We go to tell other people about what God has done for us. We go to love and to serve the Lord. And we come back again, next Sunday!

Where do we do these marvelous deeds? Where do we gather on Sunday to be the church, to listen to the word, to ask for God's help, to offer bread and wine, to give thanks and praise, to share in the meal of Jesus' great sacrifice for us? We gather in the house that we call by our very own name, the church.

Read all about the house that we call the church in the next chapter.

When we eat this bread
and drink this cup,
we proclaim your death,
Lord Jesus,
until you come in glory.

Finding Your Way Around

We are baptized. We belong to a community of people called "church." We give our own name to the house where we gather. The building is called "church," too.

Because the people called "church" gather in the house called "church," something very special happens. God lives there, too. Think about it. God made the sun and moon and stars and earth. God made the mountains and the forests and the deserts and the oceans. We can find God in all of these places.

But God says, "I will live where my people gather." And so the church building, the house of the church people, is also the house of God. Our house is God's house! God's house is our house! How wonderful!

We must love our church building and take good care of it. We must make it beautiful and keep it clean. Our church can be a place where we peek into heaven. Our church can be a sign of the holy place that the Bible tells us is so lovely, the New Jerusalem, where all people will live in peace:

Then I saw the New Jerusalem, that holy city, coming down from God in heaven. It was like a bride dressed in her wedding gown and ready to meet her husband. I heard a loud voice shout from the throne:

"God's home is now with his people. He will live with them and they will be his own."

The glory of God made the city bright. It was dazzling and crystal clear like a precious jasper stone. The city had a high and thick wall with twelve gates, and each one of them was guarded by an angel. On each of the gates was written the name of one of the twelve tribes of Israel. The city was built on twelve foundation stones. On each of the stones was written the name of one

We catch a peek
of the New Jerusalem
in our church building.
Right here in our neighborhood.

Write the name of one place where you find God:

....

Tape a photograph of that place, or draw a picture of it, in this box.

of the Lamb's twelve apostles. Each of the twelve gates was a solid pearl. The streets of the city were made of pure gold, clear and crystal. I did not see a temple there. The Lord God All-Powerful and the Lamb were its temple. And the city did not need the sun or the moon. The glory of God was shining on it, and the Lamb was its light.

In our church building, we catch a peek of this New Jerusalem. Right here in our neighborhood. In and near our homes. In and near our school. In and near our stores and playgrounds. Right here, for us.

then I saw the NEW JeRusaLem that hoLY CITY coming DOWN fRom GOD in HEAVEN

it was Like a BRIDE DRESSED in HER WEDDING GOWN and ReaDy to meet HER HUS-BanD

And not just for us. For all people. God welcomes everybody into this house. We must welcome them, too.

Do you know your way around the church? Have you been in all of the corners and closets? Have you looked at things close up and from far away? Read this chapter in church, as you walk around and look.

Go to the main door

Is it big and heavy? Can you see through it? Does it have decoration on it? Remember that Jesus said, "I am the door to heaven." The door is where we welcome people to come inside: babies and others to be baptized, visitors from other churches, the bodies of Christians who have died. In the box, draw a picture of your church's doors.

> **Draw the doors here**

Go to the place where people gather before Mass

In some church buildings it's a small place. In other church buildings it's a large room. A Greek name for the gathering space is the *narthex*. Here, we greet each other before we worship. Here, we may leave canned goods for hungry people or Christmas presents for children who have no family. Here we may buy a raffle ticket from the usher. Here we can see signs about all the things our parish does after Mass: bake sales and car washes and religion classes and spaghetti dinners.

Remember that the Mass helps us do all of these things in love.

> **Make a list of the things that you find in the gathering space:**
>
> ....
>
> ....
>
> ....
>
> ....
>
> ....
>
> ....
>
> ....
>
> ....

Go to the baptismal font

Put your hand in the water and make the sign of the cross on yourself.

Here is where we were born the second time. First, we were born in the hospital or maybe at home. Then, our

baptismal font

moms and dads and our godfathers and godmothers brought us here. In this holy water we were born again. We became children of God. We became Christians, members of the church.

When a Christian dies, his or her body is placed in a coffin and brought to the church's house for the last time. Water from the font is sprinkled on the coffin to remind everyone: This person is baptized. This person belongs to God. This person has gone home.

Near the font, find the big Easter candle. Now find the place where the holy oils are kept. This cupboard is called an **ambry**. In it are the three jars of holy oils, including the oil that smells sweet like perfume, the holy **chrism**.

The **font** is a holy place. Remember this when you pass by it or see it.

Go to where the people sit and stand

Go to the back and to the front. Go to the sides. Find the place where your family sits. Does the room look different from different places? Where do the servers sit? Where do the priest and deacon sit?

On these benches or chairs, the holy people who are the church sit. In this place, the holy people who are the church stand. Here the people sing songs of joy. Here they listen to God's word. Here they tell God that they are sorry. Here they ask God for help. Here they give God thanks and praise.

Where the people sit and stand is a holy place. Remember this. Help keep this place clean. If you find lost things here — hats or gloves or keys or glasses — give them to the ushers.

Go to the altar

The **altar** is the heart of our church building. Around this table we gather to remember Jesus, just as he told us to do. On this holy table we place our bread and wine. At this table we give God thanks and praise for all good things, for Jesus. Over this table the Holy Spirit hovers like a bird, but invisible. From this table we are fed with the bread that is Christ's body, with the wine that is Christ's blood. From this table we go to share God's love with everyone, every day and everywhere.

Some altars are made of wood — just like the table where Jesus ate the last supper, just like the cross on which he died. Some altars are made of stone — just like the one that Jacob set up on the morning after he dreamed about God coming to earth, just like the one that was rolled away from the tomb when Jesus rose from the dead. What is your altar made of — wood or stone?

The altar is a sign that Jesus is with us. Jesus is called "Christ" because he was anointed with the Holy Spirit. We are called "Christians" because at our baptism, we too were anointed with the Holy Spirit. The priest rubbed holy chrism on our heads. The Holy Spirit came into our hearts.

Before the altar was used for the first time, the bishop came and rubbed the holy chrism on it, to make the altar like Christ.

The altar is like Christ. That is why the priest and deacon kiss the altar at the beginning and the end of Mass. That is why we bow to the altar slowly and carefully when we come into the room. These actions show our love for Jesus and help us love him more.

Only these things are put on the altar: the gospel book, **The Roman Missal,** the cup, the plate of bread, the

> The altar is like Christ. That is why we bow to the altar slowly and carefully when we come into the room.

flagon of wine. We should not put song sheets, song books, papers, flowers or other things on the altar.

The altar is a holy table. Remember this when you pass by it or see it. Remember to bow before the altar when you enter the church, before you take your seat. Bow before the altar again before you leave.

Go to the ambo

The **ambo** is the holy place where the lector reads God's word to God's people. Moses went up a mountain to listen to God and bring back the Ten Commandments to the people. Jesus went up a mountain to teach the Beatitudes. The gospel is such good news that we want to shout it from the rooftops! The ambo is our mountain, our rooftop. It is the place where we speak God's word.

Here we tell the story of how God created the sun and the moon and the stars. Here we tell the story of how God called Abraham and Sarah. Here we tell the story of how God saved the people from slavery in Egypt, of how Moses parted the Red Sea and how Miriam led the people dancing and singing on the other side. Here we tell the story of the prophets who spoke for God. Here we tell the story of how God became one of us in Jesus, of how Jesus ate and drank with us and taught us how to live. And here we tell the story of how Jesus died on the cross, rose from the dead, ascended

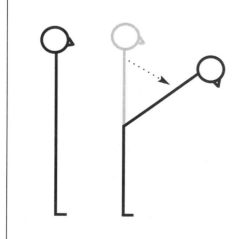

> Stand in front of the altar. See Jesus standing there. Bend slowly from your waist. Don't bend your neck. When you are bent over, look at the floor. Stay bent over for a moment. Then slowly stand up straight. This is a bow.

altar

ambo

into heaven and sent the Holy Spirit. And here we will keep telling these stories until Jesus comes again at the end of the world.

The ambo is a holy place because God's word is spoken there. We use the ambo only for God's word, for preaching and for the prayers of the faithful. Other things are said from somewhere else.

When you see the ambo, remember Jesus on the mountain teaching.

Look at the area around the altar and the ambo

Maybe the floor beneath the altar and the ambo is raised up a few steps. Maybe it looks like the stage in the school auditorium. It is not a stage, though. The floor is raised up so that people can see the altar and the ambo. The area around the altar and the ambo is sometimes called the **sanctuary**. Sometimes the priest's chair and the deacon's chair are in the sanctuary, too.

Look around for a small table or shelf

This table or shelf is called a **credence table.** Here is where you will put things before Mass — things that will be used during the Mass. They sit on

> Here we tell the story
> of how Jesus died
> on the cross,
> rose from the dead,
> ascended into heaven
> and sent the Holy Spirit.
> Here we will
> keep telling these stories
> until Jesus comes again.

the credence table until the servers bring them to the altar or the priest's chair. They are taken back to the credence table after they are used.

Find another small table. Look near the door, or in the aisle near the people's seats. This table is called the **gifts table.** On this table we put the bread and the wine before it is carried to the altar.

Go to the place where the tabernacle is

The **tabernacle** is probably in its own room, called a chapel. If there isn't a separate chapel, then the tabernacle is in the sanctuary. When Mass is over, the eucharistic bread that was not eaten is placed in the tabernacle. It is kept there so that ministers may take the eucharist to people who cannot come to church — sick people and old people who cannot come out of their houses, people who are in jail and people who are in trouble. The eucharist is also kept in the tabernacle so that we can pray in front of so great a gift.

Look for the candle in the glass burning near the tabernacle. Sometimes the glass around the candle is red. This candle burns all the time, to help us remember that Christ is here.

Remember how we bow to the altar to show our love for Jesus and to learn to love him more? We do something like that in front of the tabernacle, too. We **genuflect.** Instead of bowing at the waist, we look at the tabernacle and bend both knees. One knee touches the floor. Try it now.

Put one foot behind you a little and bend your toes. Let the knee on that leg gently touch the floor. The other knee will bend a little, too. Genuflect slowly. Keep your back straight and your eyes on the tabernacle. Then slowly stand up straight.

Go to the sacristy

A **sacristy** is a room to prepare all the things we need for Mass. Some churches have more than one. In the next chapter, we will see what is inside the sacristy. And we will learn the names of all the things that God's people use to worship God.

In Closets and Cupboards

In a house, there is a place to prepare the meal and another place to eat it. In a big house, the place to prepare the meal is the kitchen, and the place to eat it is the dining room. In a little house, the place to prepare the meal may be the countertop or the stovetop, and the place to eat is a table.

Houses have closets, too — places to hang up clothes and put away toys and tools.

The house of the church has rooms for preparation and rooms for hanging up clothes and putting away the holy things that God's holy people use to worship God. Some churches have one room, and other churches have more than one. How many rooms for preparation does your church have? Go to these rooms as you read this chapter, and find all the things that are listed here.

The Sacristy

The room where the things used in worship are kept is called the **sacristy**. The person who helps take care of and prepare all the things in the sacristy is called the **sacristan**. Sometimes many people help with this job. Does your church have a sacristan and other helpers? What are their names?

If a church has more than one sacristy, sometimes the sacristies have names. One may be called "the servers' sacristy" because that's where the servers hang up their coats and put on their robes. The other may be called "the priests' sacristy" because that is where the priests' robes are kept. One sacristy may be called "the vesting room" because that is the room where all the ministers put on their robes. The other sacristy may be called "the work sacristy" because that is where all the other things besides the robes are kept and prepared. What are the sacristies in your church called?

Find the light switches and the switch to turn on the microphones. Someone else will probably take care of this. But you should know where the switches are in case the presider asks you to go and turn something on.

Getting dressed to serve

Go to the sacristy where the servers' robes are kept. The long white robe is called an **alb.** (Sometimes servers wear a long black or red robe called a **cassock** and then a shorter white robe, called a **surplice**, over the cassock.) The alb is a reminder that we are baptized. When each of us was baptized, even if we were little babies, after the water was poured and after our heads were anointed with chrism, a white robe was put on us. The white robe reminds us that baptism washed us clean and gave us a new life. The Bible says that all the people who belong to God wear robes that shine like the sun.

Find an alb that fits you well. Try it on. The end of it should not touch the floor or make you trip. But it should cover your legs! Some servers wear a special belt with the alb. The belt is made of rope and is called a **cincture**.

Practice walking, bowing, genuflecting, sitting down and standing up with the alb on. Practice walking up and down steps with the alb on. (Watch out for the end of the alb when you go up steps or stand up from sitting down — don't let it get under your toes!)

Always put your alb on and take it off carefully. Always remember to hang it up after Mass. Handle and wear the alb with respect. It is a sign of holy baptism.

Who washes the albs? Ask your leader. Maybe you and your parents will take turns bringing the albs home to wash and dry them. Maybe the sacristan does this.

Go to where the robes for the priest and deacon are kept.

Albs for everyone!

Anyone who is baptized may wear an alb. The white dress that the bride wears at her wedding is like a very fancy alb. Sometimes the readers wear albs. Sometimes the communion ministers do. Sometimes the cantor does, too. Sometimes members of the choir wear albs or they wear robes of a different color. Sometimes these ministers wear their Sunday clothes and do not put an alb on over them.

The priest and the deacon wear an alb over their Sunday clothes and put other robes on over the alb. They may fasten their albs with a cincture around their waists.

More clothes for the priest and deacon

Both the priest and the deacon wear a **stole** around their necks. This is a long narrow prayer shawl, like the prayer shawl that Jesus wore. The priest wears the stole with both ends hanging down in front. The deacon wears the stole over the left shoulder and attached at the right side, with one end crossing over the front and one end crossing over the back, sort of like a Scout's sash.

The deacon may wear an outer garment called a **dalmatic**. It is like a jacket with big sleeves.

dalmatic and stole

The priest will wear an outer garment over the alb and stole called a **chasuble**. The word means "little house" because the chasuble looks like a tent!

Sometimes a priest or other minister will wear a special cape called a **cope**. A special prayer shawl that

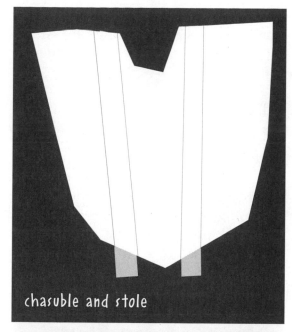
chasuble and stole

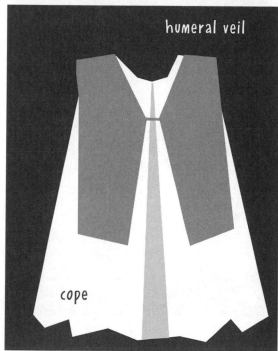
humeral veil

cope

wraps around the shoulders is called a **humeral veil**. The humeral veil is not used at Mass, but at other times.

Colors like the rainbow

Look in the closet where the chasubles and dalmatics are hung, or in the drawers where they are laid out flat. How many colors do you find?

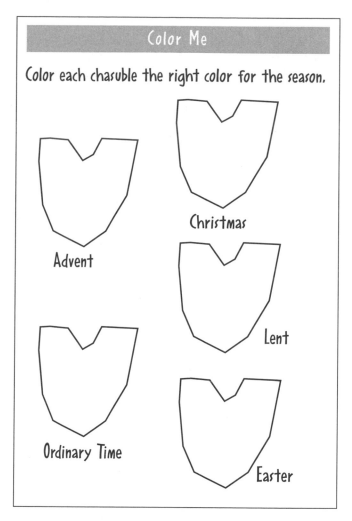

Color Me

Color each chasuble the right color for the season.

Advent

Christmas

Ordinary Time

Lent

Easter

The stole, dalmatic and chasuble have certain colors for certain times. Violet is for Advent and for Lent, and sometimes for funerals. White is for Christmas and for Easter, for special days of Jesus, Mary and the saints, and for funerals. Red is for special days of Jesus, the Holy Spirit and the **martyrs** — people who were killed for believing in Jesus. Green is for the days that we call Ordinary Time — not because they are boring, but because we count them by numbers. (Have you learned about ordinal numbers in math class yet? *Ordinal* means "counting.") Sometimes gold or silver or other special colors are used for Easter and other very important days. Sometimes rose-colored vestments are used on the

alb	the priest wears one hanging down in the front; the deacon wears one pinned on the side
cincture	baptism's robe
stole	the priest wears this outer garment
chasuble	a belt
dalmatic	this garment goes on the coffin to remind us of baptism's robe
pall	the deacon wears this outer garment

Third Sunday in Advent and the Fourth Sunday in Lent.

The bishop's stuff

The **bishop** wears the same kind of clothes that the priest does, since the bishop is a priest too. But the bishop wears some special jewelry: a ring on his finger and a cross on a chain around his neck. And the bishop wears two special hats: a beanie called a **zuchetto**, and a tall, pointed hat called a **miter**. The bishop also carries a staff like a shepherd's. (Because the bishop is our shepherd!) The staff is called a **crosier**. When the bishop comes, one server will have to hold the miter when the bishop takes it off to pray. Another server may have to hold the zuchetto, too, but usually the bishop's secretary does that. Another server holds the

crosier when the bishop needs to have both hands free. These things are not in the sacristy. The bishop brings them with him.

On the coffin

When a Christian dies, the body is brought to church in a **coffin**. A white robe is placed on the coffin. We call this robe the **pall**. The pall reminds us of an alb, and as the person is brought to the church for the last time, the pall reminds us that the dead person is baptized, a member of the body of Christ. We believe that this person, even though he or she has died, will be alive with Jesus forever because she or he is baptized, and ate the bread of life and drank from Christ's cup. Do you know where the pall is kept? Find it and look at it. See if it has any decorations on it.

pall

Tablecloths and Napkins

The church people aren't the only ones who wear special clothes for worship. The church building does, too! There are banners and tapestries that hang on the walls or from the rafters. And because the altar is our holy table, we have special tablecloths for it. Find in the sacristy the drawers that hold the altar cloths. You will not have to do anything with the **altar cloths**—putting them on is the sacristan's job. But take a look at how beautiful they are.

There are some other cloths that you will have to set out and bring back in. Can you find all these cloths?

The **corporal** is the small placemat that goes over the altar cloth. The word *corporal* comes from a Latin word that means "body." That's because this is the cloth that the body and blood of Christ rests on before it is shared. Sometimes the corporal is folded into nine squares. Find the drawer that the corporals are kept in.

The **purificators** are the napkins that we use to wipe the cups that hold the blood of Christ. They are usually folded in half. We use one purificator for each cup. Find the drawer that the purificators are kept in.

The cardboard square that is covered with linen is called a **pall.**

(That's the same name as the baptismal robe that is placed on the coffin, too. Don't get confused!) The pall is sometimes placed on top of the chalice to keep bugs and dust out of the delicious wine that becomes the blood of Christ.

After Mass, the corporal might be clean enough to use again. So when it is brought back to the sacristy, it can go back in the drawer. The purificators always have to be washed. Sometimes the sacristan or the ministers of communion will take care of the purificators. But sometimes the server is supposed to bring them into the sacristy and put them in the sink or a special washtub so that they can soak until they are washed. Ask your sacristan or leader what you should do with the purificators.

Finger towels or **hand towels** are also in the sacristy. They are used to

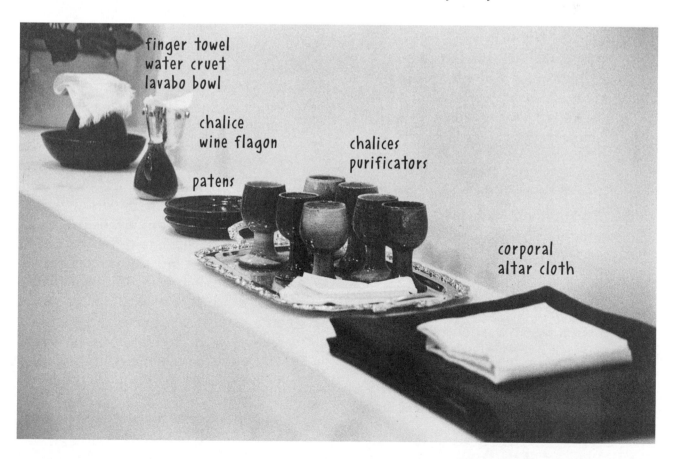

finger towel
water cruet
lavabo bowl

chalice
wine flagon

chalices
purificators

patens

corporal
altar cloth

Chalices are the beautiful cups that we use to share the wine that is the blood of Christ. One chalice is put on the altar when the gifts are prepared. The other chalices, usually on a tray, are brought to the altar before the breaking of the bread.

The wine that we offer to God is put in a beautiful vessel called a **flagon** or **cruet**. Another flagon or cruet —usually smaller—holds water that is mixed with the wine. Only the big flagon with wine is placed on the altar.

The plate that holds the bread that we offer to God is sometimes called a **paten**. If the vessel that holds the bread is more like a bowl than a plate, it is called a **ciborium**. Sometimes the ciborium has a lid.

A **pyx** is a small container used to carry the body of Christ to people who are sick at home or in the hospital, or to people who are in a nursing home or in jail.

A large vessel for holding and showing the body of Christ for prayer after Mass is called a **monstrance**. Inside the monstrance is a smaller glass container called a **lunette**.

dry the priest's hands before the great prayer of thanks. It is an old custom from before the time of Jesus to wash your hands before praying to God! They are also used to clean up after anointing people who have been baptized or confirmed. Find the drawer where these towels are kept.

Other towels are used to dry people off after the water bath of baptism. Still others are used when we wash each other's feet on Holy Thursday, like Jesus did on the night before he died.

Holy Dishes, Holy Meal

In your house, do you have a set of special dishes that you use only on Thanksgiving Day and other special days? In the house of the church, we use our best cups and plates for the Lord's supper. Servers often help by setting out the holy dishes before Mass and then by bringing them back to the sacristy after Mass. Learn the names of the holy dishes that we use. Can you find them in the sacristy?

More Containers

Another bowl is used for washing hands. Sometimes this is called the **lavabo bowl**. The word *lavabo* means "I will wash." A pitcher of water goes with this bowl. It is an old custom from before the time of Jesus to wash your hands before saying an important prayer. Servers should wash their hands even before they come to church!

Sometimes the priest and ministers sprinkle the people with holy water that comes from the baptismal font. There is a beautiful bowl or special bucket for this. Either a branch from a tree or a metal sprinkler is used to sprinkle the holy water on the holy people. The metal sprinkler is called the **aspergillum**. That's a funny name to say and remember!

When we burn incense to fill the room with perfumed smoke, we use a big ceramic bowl filled with sand or pebbles, or we use a smaller metal bowl on a chain. The bowl for burning the incense is called a **thurible**. The bowl that the grains of incense are kept in before they are burned is called a **boat**. (This isn't the only bowl that's called a boat. Does your mom have a gravy boat with her Thanksgiving dishes?) In the boat is a spoon.

Can you find all of these containers in the sacristy?

Things We Use Up

The vestments and cloths, the cups and containers — these we use again and again. So we must take good care of them. Some things we use up in our worship of God. These supplies are stored in one of the sacristies or workrooms. Go find where each of these things is kept, in case you are ever sent to fetch some of it.

Look for the *bread* and the *wine.* The bread might be stored in a cupboard. Or maybe different people in the parish make it and bring it to Mass. Some of the wine may be in a refrigerator in the sacristy. More bottles may be in a closet or cupboard. Do you know where the bread and wine are kept?

Candles are kept in a cupboard or closet, too. Servers usually do not have to change the candles. The sacristan

does that. But pay attention to where they are kept. One special kind of candle is a candle in a jar. This is called a *vigil light,* and it burns for seven days before it goes out. We keep this kind of candle burning all the time near the tabernacle. It reminds us that Christ is present in the eucharist in the tabernacle. Sometimes we also burn seven-day candles near images of Jesus, Mary and the saints. We light the candle, say a prayer and go. But the candle keeps burning and makes our prayer last longer. Sometimes we burn seven-day candles in November to remember all of the people who have died in the past year. The flame keeps burning to remind us that we keep loving the person who has died.

Besides the candles, make sure you find the candle lighting pole, the extinguisher, the wicks and the matches. Watch as your leader shows you how to use the candle pole. Practice using it to light the candles. Practice using the extinguisher to put out the candles.

Near the thurible, find the packages of charcoal and the box of incense grains. The incense charcoal is like what we use in a barbecue, only smaller. The incense grains are made of sticky stuff that comes out of trees. It hardens into grains. But when it is put on the burning coal, it melts and lets out its sweet smell.

You can help by telling the priest or sacristan whenever you use up the last bit of any of these things. Then they know they need to get more for the next liturgy.

Good Books, Holy Books

Finally, find where the books are kept. The two most important books

Match the name of the book with what is in it:

lectionary   hymns and songs

book of the gospels   gospel readings

Roman Missal   the Bible readings for
                              Mass

hymnal   the prayers for Mass

for Mass are the lectionary and the sacramentary.

The **lectionary** is the book of readings. It is like a rearranged Bible. It gives us a little portion of the Bible for every day of the year and for special occasions, too. It holds the words of God, the words of Jesus. The lector usually takes care of this book. We treat the lectionary with great care. We never throw it around, or put it on the floor, or treat it like it's just any old book.

Sometimes the gospel, the words and works of Jesus, are in a separate book from the lectionary. This is called the **book of the gospels**. Another name for this book is the **evangelary**. Usually the deacon takes care of this book. We must treat this book with the same care and respect as we treat the lectionary.

The lectionary and the book of the gospels are very important to us. That is why after reading the gospel story, the priest or deacon kisses the book.

The book of prayers is called the **sacramentary**. It has many ribbons in it: These are bookmarks. The words in the sacramentary are the words that we use to talk to God. They are important words. Some of them we sing or say over and over again: "Glory to God," "Holy, holy, holy," "We believe in one God." Some of them change day by day: the opening prayer, the prayer over the gifts, the prayer after communion. This book is important to us, too. We treat it carefully, never tossing it around, never putting it on the floor. We should make sure that we hold and carry this book with clean hands so that it doesn't get dirty and so that it will last a long time. The sacramentary is the book that servers take care of and hold.

We also have books for the various rites we celebrate. Find and look at the baptism book, the funeral book and the wedding book. We use these books when we baptize at Mass, when we witness the marriage vows of two of our parishioners, when we say good-bye to someone who has died. We use these books along with the lectionary and the sacramentary.

Books with songs and music, books for writing the names of the dead, books that hold our petitions (the favors that we ask of God) also may be in the cupboard. What do you find in your sacristy?

Serving as a Team

Have you ever played a team sport? Played a musical instrument in a band or orchestra? Danced with a dance group? If so, you know what it is like to be part of a team. Each one of the team, the orchestra, the dance group, plays a part, does a job, so that the whole group wins, sounds good, moves well. What would happen if you were supposed to play second base but decided to run after fly balls to left field? Or what would happen if you tried to play the flute part on the drum? Or what would happen if in the middle of the ballet, you started tap dancing?

At the liturgy, the whole assembly is a team, working together with Christ to give God thanks and praise. Together, all of the ministers who serve the assembly are a team, too. It's important that the servers act as a team.

On a baseball team or in a dance company, each one has a position. In an orchestra, each one has an instrument. Just as the members of a team or orchestra have names for their positions or instruments, there are names for the servers. Since every parish is slightly different, your leaders may give you different names. If so, write them next to these names.

Learn these positions one at time. Don't just read about them — practice them in church. And practice them over and over again until you are comfortable serving in the assembly.

In some instances, depending on how many servers are scheduled or show up, you may have to take more than one position. This is just like when not enough kids show up to play baseball, so the one covering second base has to be shortstop, too.

See the little picture for each serving position? You will see them again throughout the book. The picture is like a team's letter. Whenever you see the picture, you'll know which server's job is being explained.

Cross & Book ....

Candle 1 ....

Candle 2 ....

Thurifer ....

Can you guess what each server carries? You probably can guess the first three! But what do you think the server named "thurifer" carries? Guess!

Turn the page to see if you are right.

Answer: The thurifer carries the thurible, the bowl for burning incense. If thurifer is too hard to remember, just think "incense."

Cross & Book

As the name says, this server carries the cross in the processionals and later holds the book of the prayers, *The Roman Missal,* when the priest or deacon prays. The lectors take care of the other book, the lectionary.

Before Mass begins, take the cross to where the procession will start. Carry it upright and carefully, even before and after Mass.

(If the processional cross in your church is too large for you to carry, someone else — another server or an adult — may carry it instead. In that case, you take care of the book, and skip the parts about the cross.)

When incense is used, the thurifer goes first. Otherwise the crossbearer leads the procession. The two servers carrying candles either walk on either side of you, or walk together a little bit behind you.

Walk slowly, carefully. Carry the cross high. Sing the song the people are singing if you know it. When you reach the altar, stop for a moment, look at the altar and bow your head. But don't lower the cross, and don't bow your body. Move aside and either put the cross in its place right away, or wait until the other ministers all catch up so that you will all move at the same time. Your leader will tell you which way your parish does this. When you put the cross in its stand,

put it down gently. Make sure that it is standing up straight before you go to your seat. Remember: When you are not holding or carrying something, fold your hands!

For more on carrying the cross, see pages 87 and 88. Read "Carrying the Cross" from time to time to help you remember how good it is to carry the cross into the assembly.

At your seat, do what the assembly does: Sing the song (pick up the hymnal or song sheet on your seat and use it), make the sign of the cross, say the responses.

After the Glory to God is sung (or said), bring *The Roman Missal* to the priest. (Sometimes, the Glory to God is not used. In that case, after the priest says, "May almighty God have mercy on us . . ." and the people answer "Amen!", then you bring the book to the presider.) Carry the book upright with both hands, at chest height, over your heart. (Not over your head — the lector carries the lectionary like that, but we carry *The Roman Missal* over our heart.) Don't sling it under your arm like a school book.

Open the book to the correct ribbon and hold the book steady for the presider to say the prayer. Either you or the priest may close the book when the prayer is finished. Then walk back to your seat, carrying the book at chest height, just like before.

Don't put *The Roman Missal* on the floor. If there is no place on the credence table for it or no room to rest it on the bench next to you, hold it in your lap. But don't fuss with it. For more on holding the book, see pages 89–91. Read "Holding the Book" from time to time to remind yourself how good it is to hold the book.

During the readings, listen carefully to the word of God. Do what the rest of the assembly does: Sit up tall, listen, say the responses, sing the psalm, sing the acclamation, stand up tall.

When the assembly sits and it is time for the collection and preparation of the gifts of bread and wine, carry the book to the altar. Carry the book upright at chest height. Place it carefully on the altar off to one side. Open it to the correct ribbon, or leave it closed for the deacon or priest to open. Fold your hands. Step back. Bow to the altar. Walk back to your place.

Do what the rest of the assembly does as Mass continues: Sing and respond to the prayers, listen carefully, stand and sit and bow and kneel.

The deacon or priest may close the book before the breaking of the bread and place it to the side. If so, you can go (with hands folded!) and bring it back to your seat. Carry the book upright at chest height. Leave it at your place when you receive communion. If the priest needs the book all the way through the breaking of the bread, then while the assembly is receiving communion, go with folded hands and take the book from the altar. Carry the book upright with two hands back to your seat.

After communion, after the assembly has sat and kept silence for a while, the priest and all will stand. Now bring the book to the priest again. Carry the book upright with two hands at chest height. Open the book to the correct ribbon and hold it steady for the priest or deacon to say the prayer. The priest or deacon may also need the book to give the final blessing. You or the presider may close the book when the prayer or blessing is finished. Then walk back to your seat, carrying the book at chest height just like always.

Put *The Roman Missal* down carefully. Fold your hands. Go to the cross. Don't be poky, but don't run.

Carefully take the cross from its stand, and go to the front of the altar. As the other ministers bow or genuflect, you may bow your head. But don't bow your body or dip the cross. Hold the cross high. You may follow the thurifer out or you may lead the procession out. Walk slowly. If the people are singing and you know the words, you sing too. Lower the cross when you reach the end of the aisle. Carefully put the cross back in its place. You do not have to lift the cross high as you return it to its place, but never carry the cross like a broom or cane.

Your leader might give you other instructions about the cross and *The Roman Missal*. Write them in this box.

....

....

....

....

....

....

....

....

....

This name tells you two things: You carry a candle. And you're one of two; you have a partner, Candle 2. Candle 1 and Candle 2 are like twins; they stick together!

Before Mass begins, light your candle and carry it to the place where the procession will begin. Carry the candle upright so that the wax does not spill. You and Candle 2 may walk on either side of the cross. Or you may walk together a few feet behind the cross. You and Candle 2 must walk together. Before the procession starts, practice holding your candles at the same height. Maybe you are taller. Maybe you are shorter. That's OK — God makes us each unique! But the candles should be held at the same height.

For more on carrying the candle, read pages 85 and 86. Read "Lighting Candles" again from time to time to remember how good it is to carry the light of Christ into the assembly.

When you and Candle 2 reach the altar, you will do one of two things. You might spread out and wait for the other ministers to line up. Or you might stop for a moment and then go put your candle in its place. Either way, stop for a moment and look at the altar. You may bow your head, but do not bow your body or tip the candle. When you place the candle in its stand, make sure it stands up straight. Fold your hands and go to your place.

At your seat, do what the assembly does: Sing the song (pick up the hymnal or song sheet on your seat and use it), make the sign of the cross, say the responses. During the readings, listen carefully to the word of God: Sit up tall, listen, say the responses, sing the psalm, pay attention.

If your parish has a procession with the gospel book, after the second reading, after the quiet time, the priest or deacon will stand up. Stand and fold your hands. Go with Candle 2 and get your candles. Hold them at the same height. Meet the deacon or priest at the altar, and walk slowly with Candle 2. Lead the priest or deacon to the ambo. The cantor and the people will be singing the acclamation while you and the deacon or priest walk to the ambo, and if you know the words (they're usually very simple), you sing too. When you get to the ambo, you and Candle 2 stand side by side in front of it, and the priest or deacon will go up to tell the gospel. Stand up tall and listen carefully while the gospel is told. After the gospel is finished, after the people (and you!) have said "Praise to you, Lord Jesus Christ!" walk with Candle 2 slowly to put your candle in its place. Return to your seat.

Do what the rest of the assembly does: Sit up tall, listen, stand up tall, join in the saying of the creed and the response to the prayers of the faithful.

Here comes the only time that you go without Candle 2! When the assembly sits, with folded hands, walk to the credence table. (If you walk in front of the altar, bow to the altar.) Bring the chalice and the purificator to the altar. Place them on the altar, over to the side. Fold your hands. Step back. Bow to the altar. Return to your place.

When the priest or deacon moves to receive the gifts, you and Candle 2 follow. Fold your hands. You stand on one side of the presider, Candle 2 stands on the other side. Keep your hands folded. The priest or deacon will give you the wine or maybe the bread or maybe the basket of money. Hold it carefully. Wait for the priest to move to the altar, then together with Candle 2, walk to the altar. If you have the bread, give it to the priest. Fold your hands and go to the credence table with Candle 2. If you have the basket of money, place it on the floor near the altar as you learn in practice. Fold your hands and go to the credence table with Candle 2. If you have the wine, keep it and go to the credence table with Candle 2. At the credence table, if you don't have the wine, pick up the water. Go together back to the altar.

Stand up tall. Hold the water or wine carefully with two hands. If you are holding the wine, stand closer to the altar. If you are holding the water, let Candle 2 stand closer to the altar. The priest will take the wine. Fold your hands. The priest will pour some wine into the chalice, and then may give the wine vessel back to you or just the stopper for the wine vessel. Hold it. The priest will take the water, pour some into the chalice and give the water cruet back.

Go with Candle 2 back to the credence table. If you have the wine or the stopper: Put it down and take the hand towel, unfold it and hold it with both hands. If you have the water: Hold on to the cruet, and take the bowl in your other hand. If incense is used, wait until the priest is finished incensing the altar and the people, then go back with Candle 2 to the altar.

If you have the water and bowl: Hold the bowl under the priest's hands and pour water over them using your other hand. Stay put until Candle 2 is ready to go. If you have the towel: Hold it out for the priest to take. Wait to receive it back. Walk with Candle 2 back to the credence table. Put the cruet, bowl and towel down neatly off to the side. Fold the towel neatly, but quickly. Fold your hands. Return to your seat.

Do what the rest of the assembly does as Mass continues: Sing and respond to the prayers, stand and sit and bow and kneel.

After the breaking of the bread, if the wine vessel was on the altar and is now empty, the priest or deacon may put it to the side. If one of the communion ministers does not remove it, do this: Go with hands folded to the side of the altar. Bow to the altar. Take the wine vessel and return it to the credence table. Fold your hands. Return to your place.

Go to communion as the servers in your parish do. Return to your place and do as the rest of the assembly does: Sing, pray, keep silence, stand or sit or kneel.

When the priest or deacon gives the final blessing, make the sign of the cross. With folded hands, go with Candle 2 and get your candle. Line up in front of the altar. When the other ministers bow, you may bow your head, but do not bow your body or tip the candle. Walk out with Candle 2 slowly. When you reach the end of the procession, you may extinguish your candle before going to the sacristy, but don't blow wax all over! Don't tip the candle until all the wax is dried and hard.

Candle 2

 This name tells you two things: You carry a candle. And you're one of two; you have a partner, Candle 1. Candle 1 and Candle 2 are like twins; they stick together!

Before Mass begins, light your candle and carry it to the place where the procession will begin. Carry the candle upright so that the wax does not spill. You and Candle 1 may walk on either side of the cross. Or you may walk together a few feet behind the cross. You and Candle 1 must walk together. Before the procession starts, practice holding your candles at the same height.

For more on carrying the candle, read pages 85 and 86. Read "Lighting Candles" again from time to time to remember how good it is to carry the light of Christ into the assembly.

When you and Candle 1 reach the altar, you will do one of two things. You might spread out and wait for the other ministers to line up. Or you might stop for a moment and then go put your candle in its place. Either way, stop for a moment and look at the altar. You may bow your head, but don't bow your body or tip the candle. When you place the candle on its stand, make sure it stands up straight. Fold your hands and go to your place.

At your seat, do what the assembly does: Sing the song (pick up the hymnal or song sheet on your seat and use it), make the sign of the cross, say the responses. During the readings, listen carefully to the word of God: Sit up tall, listen, sing the psalm, pay attention.

If your parish has a procession with the gospel book, after the second reading, after the quiet time, the priest or deacon will stand up. Stand and fold your hands. Go with Candle 1 and get your candles. Hold them at the same height. Meet the deacon or priest at the altar, and walk slowly with Candle 1. Lead the priest or deacon to the ambo. The cantor and the people will be singing the acclamation while you and the priest or deacon walk to the ambo, and if you know the words (they're usually very simple), you sing too. When you get to the ambo, you and Candle 1 stand side by side in front of it, and the priest or deacon will tell the gospel. Stand up tall and listen carefully while the gospel is told. After the gospel is finished, after the people (and you!) have said "Praise to you, Lord Jesus Christ," walk with Candle 1 slowly to put your candle in its place. Return to your seat.

Do what the rest of the assembly does: Sit up tall, listen, stand up tall, join in the saying of the creed and the response to the prayers of the faithful.

Here comes the only time that Candle 1 goes without you! Candle 1 goes to put the chalice and purificator on the altar. You stay in your place.

When the deacon or priest moves to receive the gifts, you and Candle 1 follow. Fold your hands. You stand on one side of the priest or deacon, and Candle 1 stands on the other side. Keep your hands folded. The priest will give you the wine or maybe the bread or maybe the basket of money. Hold it carefully. Wait for the priest to move to the altar, then together with Candle 1, walk to the altar. If you have the bread, give it to the priest. Fold your hands and go to the credence table with Candle 1. If you have the money, place it on the floor near the altar as you learn in practice. Fold your hands and go to the credence table. If you have the wine, keep it and go to the credence table with Candle 1. At the credence table, if you don't have the wine, pick up the water. Go together back to the altar.

Stand up tall. Hold the water or wine carefully with two hands. If you are holding the wine, stand closer to the altar. If you are holding the water, let Candle 1 stand closer to the altar. The priest will take the wine. Fold your hands. The priest will pour some wine into the chalice and then may give the wine vessel back to you or just the stopper for the wine vessel. Hold it. The priest will take the water, pour some into the chalice and give the water cruet back.

Go with Candle 1 back to the credence table. If you have the wine or stopper: Put it down and take the hand towel, unfold it and hold it with both hands. If you have the water: Hold on to the cruet, and take the bowl in your other hand. If incense is used, wait until the priest is finished incensing the altar and the people. Go back with Candle 1 to the altar.

If you have the water and bowl: Hold the bowl under the priest's hands and pour water over them using your other hand. Stay put until Candle 1 is ready to go. If you have the towel: Hold it out for the priest to take. Wait to receive it back. Walk with Candle 1 back to the credence table. Put the cruet, bowl and towel neatly down off to the side. Fold the towel neatly, but quickly. Fold your hands. Return to your seat.

Do what the rest of the assembly does as Mass continues: Sing and respond to the prayers, listen carefully, stand and sit and bow and kneel.

After the breaking of the bread, if the wine vessel was on the altar and is now empty, the priest or deacon may put it to the side. If one of the communion ministers does not remove it, do this: Go with hands folded to the side of the altar. Bow to the altar. Take the wine vessel and return it to the credence table. Fold your hands. Return to your place.

Go to communion as the servers in your parish do. Return to your place and do as the rest of the assembly does: Sing, pray, keep silence, stand or sit or kneel.

When the priest or deacon gives the final blessing, make the sign of the cross. With folded hands, go with Candle 1 and get your candle. Line up in front of the altar. When the other ministers bow, you may bow your head, but don't bow your body or tip the candle. Walk out with Candle 1 slowly. When you reach the end of the procession, you may extinguish your candle before going to the sacristy, but don't blow wax all over! Don't tip the candle until all the wax is dried and hard.

> Your leader might give you other instructions about serving as Candle 2. Write them in this box.
>
> ....
> ....
> ....
> ....
> ....
> ....
> ....
> ....
> ....
> ....
> ....
> ....

Thurifer

 The **thurifer** is the server who carries and cares for the incense. Don't start coughing like it's a joke: Incense is holy smoke!

For more on why we use incense in church, read pages 92 – 94. And read

"Burning Incense" again from time to time to remind yourself how good it is to carry and care for the incense in God's church.

Light the coal about ten minutes before the liturgy begins. Don't hold the coal in your hand to light it. Use a pair of tongs to hold it up. Or use a wick instead of a match and touch the wick to the coal until it sparks. Then blow on it a little. Don't touch the coal after you've lit it. Even if it doesn't look red, it may still burn you. Just before the procession begins, put incense on the coal. Tap the coal with the spoon when you pour the incense.

You will be the first one in the entrance procession. If you are carrying a bowl thurible, hold it with both hands. Hold it away from your body. Gently move it back and forth to send the smoke up.

If you are carrying a thurible on a chain in procession, let it swing gently at your side. Hold your arm out so that the thurible doesn't hit your leg when you walk. If you are not carrying the boat in the other hand, put your free hand over your heart. If the people are singing and you know the words, you sing too.

When you reach the altar, stop for a moment. Bow deeply with your body and move off to the side. After all the ministers have bowed and taken their places, the priest may take the thurible from you and incense the altar. You might follow behind the priest, or you might stand off to the side and wait for the priest to finish. Your leader will tell you. When the priest gives the thurible back to you, take it to its place and put it down for now. With folded hands, go to your seat.

At your seat, do what the assembly does: Sing the song (pick up the hymnal or song sheet on your seat and use it), make the sign of the cross, say the responses. During the readings, listen carefully to the word of God. Do what the rest of the assembly does: Sit up tall, listen, sing the psalm, pay attention, stand up tall, join in the saying of the creed and the response to the prayers of the faithful.

When the priest or deacon move to receive the gifts, go get the thurible. Check on the coal — you may need to add and light a new one. If so, blow on it a bit to get it started. Bring the thurible and the boat to the altar. Stand back a bit. Let the priest finish preparing the altar and the gifts of bread and wine. Give the boat to the priest, and if the thurible has a lid, raise it. (Remember: Use the wooden knob. Never touch the metal: It's hot!) After the priest adds the incense, hand the thurible to the priest and receive the boat. You may stand back out of the way, or you may follow the presider around the altar. Your leader will tell you which way.

When the priest is done incensing the altar and the people, take the thurible and the boat back to their place. If the priest did not incense the people and it is the thurifer's job, do this: While the priest incenses the altar, put the boat back in its place. When the priest gives you the thurible, go to the group of people nearest you, bow to them (and they will bow to you). Swing the thurible in their direction at least three times. Bow again. Move to the next group of people and do the same. After you have incensed all the people in this way, go to the priest. Stand back a few feet. Bow and incense the priest, swinging the thurible at least three times. Then put the thurible in its place. Fold your hands. Go back to your place.

Do what the rest of the assembly does as Mass continues: Sing and respond to the prayers, listen carefully, stand and sit and bow and kneel.

Go to communion as the servers in your parish do. Return to your place and do as the rest of the assembly does: Sing, pray, keep silence, stand or sit or kneel.

If there is a special procession after communion, after you have prayed in your place and before the assembly is finished sharing communion, go and prepare another coal in the thurible. Stay with the thurible until after the prayers after communion and then bring the thurible and boat to the priest.

When there is no special procession, as the priest or deacon gives the final blessing, make the sign of the cross. With folded hands, go to the thurible. Add a little incense if the coal is still burning. Take the thurible and line up with the other ministers. Bow with the other ministers and lead the procession out.

If the coal is burned out, don't add another one. The Mass is ended! Leave the thurible where it is and go line up with the other ministers. Bow, and let the cross and Candle 1 and Candle 2 go first. Follow them out. If the people are singing and you know the words, you sing too.

After Mass, don't forget to clean up. Dump the ashes and hot coals from the thurible into the special container of sand in the sacristy or workroom, or outside. Your leader will show you where. Put the thurible and the boat back in their place.

Your leader might give you other instructions about serving as Thurifer. Write them in this box.

....
....
....
....
....
....
....
....
....
....
....

Serving at Sunday Mass

Remember what we learned about Sunday when we read the chapter called "Worshiping God Together" that started on page 10?

Sunday is the first day, when God began creating the heavens and the earth, separating light from darkness. Sunday is the day that Christ Jesus rose from the dead, bringing us new life. Sunday is the day that the risen Christ appeared to the disciples and said "Peace!" Sunday is the day that the Holy Spirit came like wind and like fire. Sunday is the first day that the apostles were not afraid to tell everyone about Jesus. Sunday is the day for baptism. Sunday is the day for eucharist. Sunday is the day for the church. We all come together on Sunday. We don't go to regular school. We don't go to work or we go at a different time.

It is a joy to be able to serve Mass in the Sunday assembly. When we wake up on Sunday, when we are getting ready at home to go to the house of the church, we can remember what the psalm sings about Sunday: "This is the day the Lord made, let us rejoice and be glad!"

> Remember what the psalm sings about Sunday: "This is day the Lord made, let us rejoice and be glad!"

Getting Ready to Serve

Review all the important things to remember on page 6. Remember that you have to be at church at least 20 minutes before Mass begins. There is a box on the next page where you can write down what time Mass is celebrated at your church, and what time you need to be there.

When you get to church, follow all the steps on page 6 under "Preparing."

Serving with Three or Four Servers

Because Sunday is our most important day, it is best to have at least three servers — four when incense is used. How do four servers or three servers work together as a team? Did you read the last chapter? Then you already know! When four servers or three servers work together at Sunday Mass (or on a holy day during the week that is like Sunday for us), follow the notes on pages 33–42. Know who is serving as Cross & Book, who will be Candle 1 and who will be Candle 2. When incense is used, the fourth server is Thurifer.

Sunday Mass Times

What time is Mass celebrated on Sunday in your parish?

Write the times here:

What time should you be in church?

....

....

....

....

Don't forget Saturday evening Mass time!

....

What do you do if only two servers are scheduled? Or only two show up?

If another minister carries the cross, then the two servers can be Candle 1 and Candle 2.

But then Candle 2 must carry *The Roman Missal*:

- to the priest after the Glory to God, if sung or said, or after the priest says, "May almighty God have mercy on us . . ." and the people answer, "Amen!"

- to the altar after the prayers of the faithful, when the people sit down and the collection is taken up

- to the priest after communion, after the silent prayer, when the priest stands and says, "Let us pray."

Review the notes for carrying the book on pages 89–91.

If one of you must carry the cross, neither of you will carry candles, except for the gospel procession. So we'll call you Sunday Server 1 and Sunday Server 2. Here's how you'll serve.

Sunday Server 1

 Before Mass begins, take the cross to where the procession will start. Carry it upright and carefully, even before and after Mass.

When incense is used, Thurifer goes first. Otherwise you will carry the cross and lead the procession. Sunday Server 2 will walk behind you.

Walk slowly, carefully, carrying the cross high. Sing the song if you know it. When you reach the altar, stop for a moment, look at the altar, and bow your head. But don't lower the cross, and don't bow your body. Move aside and either put the cross in its place right away, or wait until the other ministers all catch up so that you will all move at the same time. Your leader will tell you which way your parish does this.

When you put the cross in its stand, put it down gently. Make sure that it is standing up straight before going to your seat. Remember: When you are not holding or carrying something, fold your hands!

For more on carrying the cross, see pages 87–88. Read "Carrying the Cross" from time to time to help you remember how good it is to carry the cross into the assembly.

At your seat, do what the assembly does: Sing the song (pick up the hymnal or song sheet that is on your seat and use it), make the sign of the cross, say the responses. During the readings, listen carefully to the word of God: Sit up tall, listen, sing the psalm.

If your parish has a procession with the gospel book, after the second reading, after the quiet time, the priest or deacon will stand up. Stand and fold your hands. Go with Server 2 and get your candles. Hold them at the same height. Meet the priest or deacon at the altar, and walk slowly with Server 2. Sing the acclamation with the people. Lead the deacon or priest to the ambo and stand side by side with Server 2 in front of the ambo, and the priest or deacon will tell the gospel. Stand up tall and listen carefully while the gospel is told. After the gospel is finished, after the people (and you!) have said, "Praise to you, Lord Jesus Christ," walk with Server 2 slowly to put your candle in its place. Return to your seat.

Do what the rest of the assembly does: Sit up tall, listen, stand up tall, join in the saying of the creed and the response to the prayers of the faithful.

When the assembly sits for the collection and preparation of the gifts of bread and wine, with folded hands, walk to the credence table. (If you walk in front of the altar, bow to the altar.) Bring the chalice and the purificator to the altar. Place them on the altar, to the side. Fold your hands. Step back. Bow to the altar. Return to your place.

When the priest or deacon moves to receive the gifts, you and Server 2 follow. Fold your hands. You stand on one side of the deacon or priest; Server 2 stands on the other side. Keep your hands folded. The priest will give you the wine or perhaps the bread or even the basket of money. Hold it carefully. Wait for the priest to move to the altar.

If you have the bread, go to the altar and hand it to the priest. Fold your hands and go the credence table. If you have the basket of money, place it on the floor as you learned in practice. Fold your hands and go to the credence table. If you have the wine, go with Server 2 to the credence table. At the credence table, when Server 2 and you have the water and the wine, you and Server 2 go back to the altar.

Stand up tall. Hold the water or wine carefully with both hands. If you are holding the wine, you stand closer to the altar. If you are holding the water, let Server 2 stand closer to the altar. The priest will take the wine. Fold your hands. The priest will pour some wine into the chalice and then may give the wine vessel back to you or just the stopper for the wine vessel. Hold it. The priest will take the water, pour some into the chalice, and give the water cruet back.

Go with Server 2 back to the credence table. If you have the wine or the stopper: Put it down. Take the hand towel, unfold it and hold it with both hands. If you have the water: Hold on to the cruet, and take the bowl in your other hand. If incense is used, wait until the priest is finished incensing the altar and the people. Go back with Server 2 to the altar.

If you have the water and bowl: Hold the bowl under the priest's hands and pour water over them using your other hand. Stay put until Server 2 is ready to go. If you have the towel: Hold it out for the priest to take. Wait to receive it back. Walk with Server 2 back to the credence table. Put the water, bowl and towel down on the credence table, neatly, off to the side. Fold the towel neatly, but quickly. Fold your hands. Return to your seat.

Do what the rest of the assembly does as Mass continues: Sing and respond to the prayers, listen carefully, stand and sit and bow and kneel.

After the breaking of the bread, if the wine vessel was on the altar and is now empty, the priest or deacon may put it to the side. If one of the communion ministers does not remove it, do this: Go with hands folded to the side of the altar. Bow to the altar. Take the wine vessel and return it to the credence table. Fold your hands. Return to your place.

Go to communion as the servers in your parish do. Return to your place and do as the rest of the assembly does: Sing, pray, keep silence, stand or sit or kneel.

When the priest or deacon gives the final blessing, make the sign of the cross. Fold your hands. Walk to the cross. Don't be pokey, but don't run.

Carefully take the cross from its stand and go to the front of the altar. As the other ministers bow or genuflect, you may bow your head. But don't bow your body or dip the cross. Lift the cross high. You lead the procession out. Walk slowly. If the people are singing and you know the words, you sing too. Lower the cross when you reach the end of the aisle. Carefully put the cross back in its place. You do not have to lift the cross high when you return it to its place, but never carry the cross like a broom or a cane.

Sunday Server 2

 You will enter in procession walking behind the crossbearer. You should carry an open hymnal or a song sheet and sing with the assembly. (If you are not carrying a hymnal or song sheet, fold your hands!)

When you reach the altar, step to one side. Wait for the other ministers to line up. Then bow deeply with all the other ministers. Go to your seat.

At your seat, do what the assembly does: Sing the song, make the sign of the cross, say the responses.

After the Glory to God is sung or said, bring *The Roman Missal* to the priest. Sometimes, the Glory to God is not used. In that case, after the priest says, "May almighty God have mercy on us . . ." and the people answer "Amen!", then bring the book to the priest. Carry the book upright with both hands, at chest height, over your heart. (Not over your head — the lector carries the lectionary like that but we don't carry *The Roman Missal* over our heart.) Don't sling it under your arm like a school book.

Open the book to the correct ribbon and hold it steady for the priest to say the prayer. You or the priest may close the book when the prayer is finished. Then walk back to your seat, carrying *The Roman Missal* at chest height, just like before.

Don't put *The Roman Missal* on the floor. If there is no place on the credence table to put it, or no room to rest it on the bench next to you, hold it in your lap. But don't fuss with it. For more on holding *The Roman Missal*, see pages 89 – 91. Read "Holding the Book" from time to time to remind yourself how good it is to hold the book.

During the readings, listen carefully to the word of God: Sit up tall, listen, sing the psalm.

If your parish has a procession with the gospel book, after the second reading, after the quiet time, the priest or deacon will stand up. Stand and fold your hands. Go with Server 1 and get your candles. Hold them at the same height. Meet the priest or deacon at the altar, and walk slowly with Server 1. Sing the acclamation with the people. Lead the deacon or priest to the ambo and stand side by side with Server 1 in front of the ambo, and the priest or deacon will tell the gospel. Stand up tall and listen carefully while the gospel is told. After the gospel is finished, after the people (and you!) have said "Praise to you, Lord Jesus Christ" walk with Server 1 slowly to put your candle in its place. Return to your seat.

Do what the rest of the assembly does: Sit up tall, listen, stand up tall, join in the saying of the creed and the response to the prayers of the faithful.

When the assembly sits for the collection and preparation of the gifts of bread and wine, carry the book to the altar. Carry the book upright at chest height. Place it carefully on the altar off to one side. If you know which ribbon to open to, do so. But don't worry if you don't know. Leave the book closed and let the deacon or priest open it. Fold your hands. Step back. Bow to the altar. Return to your place.

When the priest and deacon move to receive the gifts, you and Server 1 follow. Fold your hands. You stand on one side of the deacon and priest; Server 1 stands on the other side. Keep your hands folded. The priest will give you the wine or perhaps the bread or even the basket of money. Hold it carefully. Wait for the priest to move to the altar. If you have the bread, go to the altar and hand it to the priest. Fold your hands and go the credence table. If you have the basket of money, place it on the floor as you learn in practice. Fold your hands and go to the credence table. If you have the wine, go with Server 1 to the credence table. At the

credence table, when Server 1 and you have the water and the wine, go back to the altar.

Stand up tall. Hold the water or wine carefully with two hands. If you are holding the wine, you stand closer to the altar. If you are holding the water, let Server 1 stand closer to the altar. The priest will take the wine. Fold your hands. The priest will pour some wine into the chalice and then may give the wine vessel back to you or just the stopper for the wine vessel. Hold it. The priest will take the water, pour some into the chalice, and give the water cruet back.

Go with Server 1 back to the credence table. If you have the wine or stopper: Put it down. Take the hand towel, unfold it and hold it with both hands. If you have the water: Hold on to the cruet, and take the bowl in your other hand. If incense is used, wait until the priest is finished incensing the altar and the people. Go back with Server 1 to the altar.

If you have the water and bowl: Hold the bowl under the priest's hands and pour water over them using your other hand. Stay put until Server 1 is ready to go. If you have the towel: Hold it out for the priest to take. Wait to receive it back. Walk with Server 1 back to the credence table. Put the water, bowl and towel neatly down off to the side. Fold the towel neatly, but quickly. Fold your hands. Return to your seat.

Do what the rest of the assembly does as Mass continues: Sing and respond to the prayers, listen carefully, stand and sit and bow and kneel.

The priest or deacon may close the book before the breaking of the bread, and place it to the side. If so, you can go (with hands folded!) and take it back to your seat at this time. Carry the book upright at chest height. Leave it at your place when you receive communion. If the priest needs the book all the way through the breaking of the bread, then while the assembly is receiving communion, go with folded hands and take the book from the altar. Carry the book upright with two hands back to your seat.

After the breaking of the bread, if the wine vessel was on the altar and is now empty, the priest or deacon may put it to the side. If one of the communion ministers does not remove it, do this: Go with hands folded to the side of the altar. Bow to the altar. Take the wine vessel and return it to the credence table. Fold your hands. Return to your place.

Go to communion as the servers in your parish do. Return to your place and do as the rest of the assembly does: Sing, pray, keep silence, stand or sit or kneel.

After communion, after the assembly has sat and kept silence for a while, the priest and all will stand. Bring the book to the priest. Carry the book upright with two hands at chest height. Open the book to the correct ribbon and hold it for the priest to say the prayer. The priest or deacon may also need the book to give the final blessing. You or the deacon or priest may close the book when the prayer or blessing is finished. Then walk back to your seat, carrying *The Roman Missal* at chest height just like always. Put *The Roman Missal* down carefully.

When the priest or deacon gives the final blessing, if you are not holding the book, make the sign of the cross. Line up with the other ministers. Carry your hymnal or song sheet and sing with the assembly. Bow with the other ministers. Walk out in procession behind Server 1 with the cross.

After Mass is done, if your parents aren't in a hurry, maybe you could stop for a minute in the tabernacle chapel or at Mary's shrine and say a quick prayer of thanks: for the gift of Jesus, for this parish community of people who love each other, for the Mass we have celebrated, for Sunday.

And if there are doughnuts and juice in the parish hall, and if it's OK with your parents, stop in and have some!

After Mass

Don't forget to clean up. See page 6.
Don't forget these important things, even after Mass when you are cleaning up:

- Bow when you pass the altar.
- Genuflect when you pass the tabernacle.
- Carry things with both hands as if you are carrying eggs.
- Don't blow out the candles; use the extinguisher.
- Hang up your alb!

Serving at Weddings

Have you ever been to a wedding before? What's it like?

Weddings are happy times. Two people love each other. Two families become one big one. There's music and flowers and later, good food to eat. There's a little sadness sometimes, too: A son or daughter leaves the house to live in a new one. Mothers and fathers are nervous and hope that their newly-married children will be safe and happy.

Baptized people get married in church because we know that marriage is a way to be with God! Married people love each other like God loves us. Christ loves the church like a groom loves his bride, like a bride loves her groom. And the Bible tells us: God is love.

It's a great joy to serve a wedding in the church. Most of the time the wedding is celebrated with a Mass. But sometimes the wedding is celebrated without Mass. But this liturgy feels like the first part of Mass, so you will know what to do.

Sometimes at weddings, because people are so excited, someone might do something silly like forget what they're supposed to do or say. If that happens, don't giggle — pretend that's what was supposed to happen. The presider, that is, the priest or deacon, will make sure that everyone gets to the right places at the right times and says the right things. (You can giggle about it after everyone has gone if you still need to.)

How Many Servers?

It's best when three servers serve a wedding (or four when incense is used). But two can do it. Because weddings are so important to the church, they are like Sunday Mass — no matter what day of the week they are on! When three servers serve, they are Cross & Book, Candle 1 and Candle 2 — just like on Sunday. So look again at pages 33–43. Candle 1 and Candle 2 have an extra job at weddings, though. See below. (When incense is used, the fourth server is Thurifer.)

When two servers are scheduled, they work like Server 1 and Server 2 for Sunday. So look again at pages 45–49. And read "The Special Part" on this page and the next for how they do the special things after the homily.

Preparing to Serve

You have at be to church early, as usual when you serve. In addition to all the things that you set up for Sunday Mass, you may have to prepare these things, too:

- a plate for the wedding rings
- the bucket of holy water and sprinkler
- an extra book besides *The Roman Missal* (the rite book)

If the wedding is not a Mass, you don't need to prepare the things for Mass like the bread, wine, chalices and so on. The priest or sacristan will tell you what to do.

Review all the other things that you need to prepare by looking again at page 6.

The Beginning

Weddings may begin a little differently than Sunday Mass. The procession of servers and presider may go the short route from the sacristy to the altar and wait there for the bride and her attendants to come up the aisle in a procession of their own. But a better way is when the procession is just like on Sunday, but with the bride and groom and their parents and friends joining the servers and presider.

No matter how it goes, remember these things:

- Don't bow your body or tip the cross or candle if you are carrying it.
- If you aren't carrying anything, fold your hands.

The Special Part: Three Servers

After the homily, the rite of marriage is celebrated.

 Cross & Book brings the rite book to the presider. You may have to hold it open for the presider. Otherwise, return to your place with hands folded.

 Candle 1 gets the plate for the wedding rings. Candle 2 gets the holy water bucket and sprinkler. You stand on either side of the presider and face the same way.

The couple getting married will exchange their vows. This is a very important moment. Pay close attention to what they say and don't fidget or look around.

One of the attendants will give the rings to the presider. The presider will place the rings on the plate and sprinkle them with holy water. Then the bride and groom exchange rings. Stand still and listen to what they say. When incense is used, the presider might incense the couple now. But your leader will tell you about this.

Stay standing next to the presider until the presider moves to the chair or to the altar. Then go put the plate and the bucket on the credence table. Fold your hands and go back to your place.

The Mass will continue as usual on Sunday. If there is no Mass, there will be some prayers, a final blessing and the procession out.

The Special Part: Two Servers

After the homily, the rite of marriage is celebrated.

 Server 1 brings the rite book to the presider. You may have to hold it open for the presider. Or you may take the plate from Server 2 and hold it. Server 2 gets the plate for the wedding rings and the holy water bucket (with the sprinkler in it). You stand on either side of the presider and face the same way.

The couple getting married will exchange their vows. This is a very important moment. Pay close attention to what they say and don't fidget or look around.

One of the attendants will give the rings to the presider. The presider will place the rings on the plate and sprinkle them with holy water. Then the bride

and groom exchange rings. Stand still and listen to what they say.

Stay standing next to the presider until the presider moves to the chair or to the altar. Then go put the rite book, the plate and the bucket on the credence table. Fold your hands and go back to your place.

The Mass will continue as usual on Sunday. If there is no Mass, there will be some prayers, a final blessing and the procession out.

After the Wedding

As you are cleaning up, the bride and groom or one of their friends may give you a small gift or an envelope of money for helping make their day so special. Don't forget to say thank you!

In some parishes, the money is collected and used to treat all the servers. So you may not get something then, but later something special will be done for all of you.

Either way is fine. And it's fine if no gift or money is given, too. We serve weddings to serve God in the church, and we don't expect any reward. Right?

Serving at Funerals

Have you ever been to a funeral? What was it like? How did you feel?

Funerals are sad times. Sometimes a person lives a long life and then dies peacefully. We are still sad. Sometimes a person has a terrible disease and suffers greatly. When this person dies, we are relieved that the suffering is over. But we are still sad because we loved this person who is now gone. Sometimes a person dies young, by accident or violence. And we are very sad and shocked. And maybe we are afraid: Could this happen to me? It's all right to have feelings like these.

> When we were baptized, we became part of Christ. What happened to Christ happens to us.

When a baptized person dies, we gather together as a church. We remember that Jesus died once. And when he died, his mother and his friends took care of him and buried him. But then he rose from the dead. He showed us that death is not the end, that love is stronger than death, that love never dies. When we were baptized, we became part of Christ. What happened to Christ happens to us. Of course, we won't see the dead person rise up out the coffin. But we know that the dead person is with God. We know that someday we will be with God, too. And on that day we will see this dead person again, and he or she will be alive in God.

How Many Servers?

It's best when four servers serve a funeral. We'll need incense! Because the funeral is so important, the funeral Mass is like a Sunday Mass for us, no matter what day of the week it is on. Three servers — or even two — can also do it.

If four of you are scheduled, serve just like on Sunday, with the fourth server being Thurifer. The beginning and end of the funeral Mass are a little different, so they are described below.

If three of you serve, Candle 1 and Candle 2 do not carry their candles at the end of Mass, but handle the incense instead.

If two of you serve, Server 1 carries the cross and Server 2 handles the incense at the end of Mass.

Sometimes the funeral is not a Mass. But then it is just like the first part of Mass so you will know how to do it.

Preparing to Serve

You have to be at church early, as usual when you serve. In addition to all the things that you set up for Sunday Mass, you may have to prepare these things, too:

- the pall, the white covering for the coffin, near the back
- the bucket of holy water and sprinkler, near the back
- an extra book besides *The Roman Missal* (the rite book)
- the Easter candle lit, in the place where the coffin will rest.

If the funeral is not a Mass, you don't need to prepare the things for Mass like the bread, wine, chalices and so on. The priest or sacristan will tell you what to do.

Review all the other things that you need to prepare by looking again at page 6.

The Beginning

The funeral will begin differently than Sunday Mass. The procession of servers and presider, that is, the priest or deacon, will go to meet the coffin at the door.

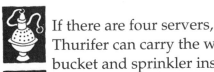 If there are four servers, Thurifer can carry the water bucket and sprinkler instead of the thurible. Cross & Book, Candle 1 and Candle 2 should all step to the side of the aisle.

 Thurifer (with the holy water) stays next to the presider. If there are three servers, the water bucket can be on a table nearby. If there are two servers, Server 1 carries the cross and Server 2 the bucket of holy water.

After the special prayers at the door, the procession moves in as it would on a Sunday.

No matter how it goes, remember these things:

- Don't bow your body or tip the cross or candle if you are carrying it.
- If you are not carrying anything, fold your hands.

The Special Part: Four Servers

The special part of the funeral comes at the end: after communion if the funeral is a Mass; after the homily and prayers of the faithful if the funeral is not a Mass.

    After communion, the presider goes and stands by the coffin. Cross & Book gives the presider the rite book, then goes and gets the cross. Candle 1 and Candle 2 get their candles. Thurifer gets the incense. Thurifer stands with the presider at one end of the coffin. Cross, with Candle 1 and Candle 2 on each side, stands a few feet back from the other end. Your leader will show you how this works in your church building.

During these prayers, the presider will incense the body of the Christian who died. This shows that we are sending this person to be with God, even if we are sad to say goodbye.

Then the procession moves to the main door. Thurifer gets behind Cross. Then Thurifer, Cross, Candle 1 and Candle 2 turn and slowly walk down the aisle. Walk very slowly, as all the people will get behind you. When you reach the door, step aside, but stay there until the body is carried out of the church.

If servers go to the cemetery for the rite of committal, your leaders will tell you what to do.

The Special Part: Three Servers

The special part of the funeral comes at the end: after communion if the funeral is a Mass; after the homily and prayers of the faithful if the funeral is not a Mass.

  After communion, the presider goes and stands by the coffin. Cross & Book gives the presider the rite book, then goes and gets the cross. Candle 1 and Candle 2 do not get candles. Candle 1 gets the thurible and Candle 2 gets the boat. They stand with the presider at one end of the coffin. Cross stands a few feet back from the other end. Your leader will show you how this works in your church building.

During these prayers, the presider will incense the body of the Christian who died. This shows that we are sending this person to be with God, even if we are sad to say goodbye.

Then the procession moves to the door. Candle 1 (with the thurible) gets behind Cross, Candle 2 (with the boat) in front. Then all three of you turn and slowly walk down the aisle: Candle 1 is first, then Cross, then Candle 2. Walk very slowly, as all the people will get behind you. When you reach the

door, step aside, but stay there until the body is carried out of the church.

If servers go to the cemetery for the rite of committal, your leader will tell you what to do.

The Special Part: Two Servers

The special part of the funeral comes at the end: after communion if the funeral is a Mass; after the homily and prayers of the faithful if the funeral is not a Mass.

  After communion, the presider goes and stands by the coffin. Server 1 gives the presider the rite book, then goes and gets the cross. Server 2 gets the thurible and boat. Server 2 stands with the presider at one end of the coffin. Server 1 stands a few feet back from the other end. Your leader will show you how this works in your church building.

During these prayers, the presider will incense the body of the Christian who died. This shows that we are sending this person to be with God, even if we are sad to say goodbye.

Then the procession moves to the main door. Server 2 gets behind Server 1. Then both of you turn and slowly walk down the aisle: Server 2 is first, then Server 1 with the cross. Walk very slowly, as all the people will get behind you. When you reach the door, step aside, but stay there until the body is carried out of the church.

If servers go to the cemetery for the rite of committal, your leader will tell you what to do.

If the servers go with the presider to the cemetery for the rite of committal, your leader will explain what to do. A server may hold the rite book for the presider. Another may hold the holy water. A third may hold the incense. A fourth may even hold the cross.

If you don't have to go to the cemetery, help with putting things away as usual. Then hurry back to school! You don't want to miss that spelling quiz or those story problems!

Prayers

Procession

Serving at Daily Mass

While Sunday is our most important day in the church, and Sunday Mass our biggest celebration of the week, Mass is often celebrated every day. If Mass cannot be celebrated on a Wednesday, say, or a Thursday, perhaps your parish has daily prayer instead. You may be asked to serve daily prayer. If so, see pages 62–66.

We also have holy days that fall on days other than Sunday. Serve Mass on a holy day just like Sunday. There'll be four or three or two of you, but follow the directions for serving Sunday Mass. Holy days are like Sunday during the week!

But how do you serve Mass on a regular Monday through Saturday?

Daily Mass with Three Servers

 If your parish has three servers assigned for daily Mass, one server is Cross & Book. But if daily Mass is in a small chapel, you may not carry the cross. Or maybe you'll carry the cross, but won't hold the book. Your leader will tell you.

 The other two servers are like Candle 1 and Candle 2 on Sunday, but you won't carry candles! There probably won't be a gospel book procession, either. So the most important thing you'll do is help with the chalice and the purificator, the water and the wine, and the washing of hands. If the people do not bring up the gifts of bread and wine, you may have to bring them to the altar from the credence table.

Do this after the prayers of the faithful when the people sit down. First Candle 1 brings over the chalice and purificator. At the same time, Candle 2 brings the plate with the bread. Both go back to the credence table and bring the wine and water, then the water and bowl and towel.

Daily Mass with Two Servers

Most likely, two servers will serve daily Mass. Let's call them Weekday Server 1 and Weekday Server 2. Even though there are two servers — and there may be only two servers at Sunday Mass, too — weekday Mass is different than Sunday. So here's how it might work.

Weekday Server 1

 Before Mass begins, take the cross to where the procession will start. Carry it upright and carefully, even before and after Mass.

Server 1 carries the cross and leads the procession. Server 2 will walk behind you. Walk slowly, carrying the cross high. Sing the song if you know it. When you reach the altar, stop for a moment, look at the altar and bow your head. But don't lower the cross, and

Find out the times and days of daily Mass in your parish, and write the schedule here:

Monday:

Tuesday:

Wednesday:

Thursday:

Friday:

Saturday:

don't bow your body. Move aside and either put the cross in its place right away or wait until the other ministers catch up so that you will all move at the same time. Your leader will tell you which way your parish does this.

When you put the cross in its stand, put it down gently. Make sure that it is standing up straight and facing the people before going to your seat. Remember: When you are not holding or carrying something, fold your hands!

If the chapel for daily Mass is small, maybe the cross is not carried in. Then you and the other server walk side by side, with hands folded. Bow to the altar. Then go to your seat.

At your seat, do what the assembly does: Sing the song (pick up the hymnal or song sheet on your seat and use it), make the sign of the cross, say the responses. During the readings, listen carefully to the word of God: Sit up tall, listen, sing the psalm, stand up tall, join in the response to the prayers of the faithful.

When the assembly sits, with folded hands, walk to the credence table. If you walk in front of the altar, bow to the altar. If the people are going to bring up the gifts, bring the chalice and the purificator to the altar. Carry them carefully. Place them to the side of the altar. Fold your hands. Step back. Bow to the altar. Return to your place.

If the people are not going to bring up the gifts, and the plate of bread is on the credence table, wait at the credence table for Server 2. Server 2 takes the plate of bread. Then bring the chalice and purificator. At the altar, after you place the chalice and purificator, with Server 2, step back and bow to the altar. Return together to your places.

If the people do bring up the gifts, when the priest moves to receive them, you and Server 2 follow. Fold your hands. You stand on one side of the priest; Server 2 stands on the other side. Keep your hands folded. The priest will give you the wine or perhaps the bread. Hold it carefully. Wait for the priest to move to the altar. If you have the bread, go to the altar and hand it to the priest. Fold your hands and go the credence table. If you have the wine, keep it and go with Server 2 to the credence table. At the credence table, when Server 2 and you have the water and the wine, go back to the altar.

Stand up tall. Hold the water or wine carefully with two hands. If you are holding the wine, stand closer to the altar. If you are holding the water, let Server 2 stand closer to the altar. The priest will take the wine. Fold your hands. The priest will pour some wine into the chalice, and then may give the wine vessel back to you or just the stopper for the wine vessel. Hold it. The priest will take the water, pour some into the chalice and give the water cruet back.

Go with Server 2 back to the credence table. If you have the wine or the stopper: Put it down and take the hand towel, unfold it and hold it with both hands. If you have the water: Hold on to the cruet, and take the bowl in your other hand. Go back with Server 2 to the altar.

If you have the water and bowl: Hold the bowl under the priest's hands and pour water over them using your other hand. Stay put until Server 2 is ready to go. If you have the towel: Hold it out for the priest to take. Wait to receive it back. Walk with Server 2 back to the credence table. Put the cruet, bowl and towel neatly down off to the side. Fold the towel neatly, but quickly. Fold your hands. Return to your seat.

Do what the rest of the assembly does as Mass continues: Sing and respond to the prayers, listen carefully, stand and sit and bow and kneel.

After the breaking of the bread, if the wine vessel was on the altar and is now empty, the priest or deacon may put it to the side. If one of the communion ministers does not remove it, do this: Go with hands folded to the side of the altar. Bow to the altar. Take the wine vessel and return it to the credence table. Fold your hands. Return to your place.

Go to communion as the servers in your parish do. Return to your place and do as the rest of the assembly does: Sing, pray, keep silence, stand or sit or kneel.

When the priest or deacon gives the final blessing, make the sign of the cross. Fold your hands. If you carried the cross in, now it is time to go to the cross to carry it out. Don't be poky, but don't run.

Carefully take the cross from its stand and go to the front of the altar. As the other ministers bow or genuflect, you may bow your head. But don't bow your body or dip the cross. Lift the cross high. You lead the procession out. Walk slowly. Lower the cross when you reach the end of the aisle. Carefully put the cross back in its place. You don't have to lift the cross high as you return it to its place, but never carry the cross like a broom or cane.

Weekday Server 2

 You will enter in procession walking behind Server 1 if the cross is carried. You should carry the open hymnal or the song sheet and sing with the assembly. (If you are not carrying the hymnal or song sheet, fold your hands!) When you reach the altar, step to one side. Wait for the other ministers to line up. Then bow deeply with all the other ministers. Go to your seat.

If the cross is not carried, walk side by side with Server 1.

At your seat, do what the assembly does: Sing the song, make the sign of the cross, say the responses.

After the priest says, "May Almighty God have mercy on us . . ." and the people answer, "Amen!", then bring the book to the priest. Carry the book upright with two hands, at chest height.

Open the book to the correct ribbon and hold it steady for the priest to say the prayer. You or the priest may close the book when the prayer is finished. Then walk back to your seat, carrying the book at chest height.

Don't put *The Roman Missal* on the floor. If there is no place on the credence table to put it, or no room to rest it on the bench next to you, hold it in your lap. But don't fuss with it.

During the readings, listen carefully to the word of God: Sit up tall, listen, sing the psalm, stand up tall, join in the response to the prayers of the faithful.

When the assembly sits, carry the book to the altar. Carry the book upright at chest height. Place it carefully on the altar off to one side. Open the book to the correct ribbon or leave the book closed and let the deacon or priest open it. Fold your hands. Step

back. Bow to the altar. Walk back to your place.

If the people are not going to bring up the gifts, and the bread is on the credence table, go to the credence table. When Server 1 brings the chalice and purificator to the altar, you bring the plate of bread. Place the bread on the altar off to one side. With Server 1, step back. Bow to the altar. Return to your place.

If the people do bring up the gifts, when the priest moves to receive them, you and Server 1 follow. Fold your hands. You stand on one side of the priest; Server 1 stands on the other side. Keep your hands folded. The priest will give you the wine or perhaps the bread. Hold it carefully. Wait for the priest to move to the altar. If you have the bread, go to the altar and hand it to the priest. Fold your hands and go the credence table. If you have the wine, keep it and go with Server 1 to the credence table. At the credence table, when Server 1 and you have the water and the wine, go back to the altar.

Stand up tall. Hold the water or wine carefully with two hands. If you are holding the wine, stand closer to the altar. If you are holding the water, let Server 1 stand closer to the altar. The priest will take the wine. Fold your hands. The priest will pour some wine into the chalice, and then may give the wine vessel back to you or just the stopper for the wine vessel. Hold it. The priest will take the water, pour some into the chalice and give the water cruet back.

Go with Server 1 back to the credence table. If you have the wine or the stopper: Put it down and take the hand towel, unfold it and hold it with both hands. If you have the water: Hold on to the cruet, and take the bowl in your other hand. Go back with Server 1 to the altar.

If you have the water and bowl: Hold the bowl under the priest's hands and pour water over them using your other hand. Stay put until Server 1 is ready to go. If you have the towel: Hold it out for the priest to take. Wait to receive it back. Walk with Server 1 back to the credence table. Put the water, bowl and towel neatly down off to the side. Fold the towel neatly, but quickly. Fold your hands. Return to your seat.

Do what the rest of the assembly does as Mass continues: Sing and respond to the prayers, listen carefully, stand and sit and bow and kneel.

The priest or deacon may close the book before the breaking of the bread, and place it to the side. If so, you can go (with hands folded!) and take it back to your seat at this time. Carry the book upright at chest height. Leave it at your place when you receive communion. If the priest needs the book through the breaking of the bread, while the assembly is receiving communion, go with folded hands and take the book from the altar. Carry the book upright with two hands back to your seat.

After the breaking of the bread, if the wine vessel was on the altar and is now empty, the priest or deacon may put it to the side. If one of the communion ministers does not remove it, do this: Go with hands folded to the side of the altar. Bow to the altar. Take the wine vessel and return it to the credence table. Fold your hands. Return to your place.

Go to communion as the servers in your parish do. Return to your place and do as the rest of the assembly does: Sing, pray, keep silence, stand or sit or kneel.

After communion, after the assembly has sat and kept silence for a while, the priest and all will stand. Bring the book to the priest. Carry the book upright with two hands at chest height. Open the book to the correct ribbon and hold it steady for the priest to say the prayer. The priest or deacon may also need the book to give the final blessing. You or the priest or deacon may close the book when the prayer or blessing is finished. Then walk back to your seat, carrying *The Roman Missal* at chest height. Put *The Roman Missal* down carefully.

When the priest or deacon gives the final blessing, if you are not holding the book, make the sign of the cross. Line up with the other ministers. Carry your hymnal or song sheet and sing with the assembly. Bow with the other ministers. Walk out in procession behind Server 1 with the cross.

After Mass is done, maybe you could stop for a minute in the tabernacle chapel or Mary's shrine and say a prayer of thanks: for Jesus, for this parish community of people who love each other, for the Mass we have celebrated.

After Mass

Don't forget to clean up. See page 6.
Don't forget these important things, even after Mass when you are cleaning up:

- Bow when you pass in front of the altar.
- Genuflect when you pass the tabernacle.
- Carry things with both hands as if you are carrying eggs.
- Don't blow out candles; use the extinguisher.
- Hang up your alb!

Serving at Daily Prayer

Sometimes, instead of or addition to daily Mass, we gather together to praise God and ask for God's help in the morning or when the sun sets. These liturgies are called **Morning Prayer** and **Evening Prayer**. Because they are celebrated at specific times of the day, they are part of the church's rites called the Liturgy of the Hours.

Singing the psalms and canticles—the songs that are in the Bible—is an important part of the Liturgy of the Hours. Another important part is asking for God's help—not just for ourselves, but for people everywhere. Even people we don't like!

Morning Prayer

Morning Prayer is sometimes called by its Latin name, *lauds,* meaning "praises." When we wake up, we are sleepy but happy to be alive, happy to have another day. We rise out of bed like Jesus rose from the grave. So we come together, turn to God and sing songs of praise. And we ask God to help us live this day as followers of Jesus.

At Morning Prayer we usually sing Psalm 63, saying that we thought about God all night and now promise to live this day right. We also sing the song that Zechariah sang when God told him that he and Elizabeth would have a baby, John the Baptist. They were old people, and Zechariah was so surprised and happy that he sang a song that begins, "Blessed be the God of Israel!" This song is called by its Latin name, the *Benedictus* (ben-a-DIC-tus). If we don't sing Zechariah's song, we sing the song of the angels: "Glory to God in the highest!"

At Morning Prayer, we might use water to bless each other with, and incense to send our prayers up to God with the smoke. The servers will help with this. And one of the servers will hold the book for the prayers that the presider says.

Evening Prayer

Evening Prayer is sometimes called by its Latin name, *vespers.* This word in Latin is the name of the first star that comes out—a sign that day is done and the night is coming. When we finish school, when we finish our chores and our homework, when we get ready to eat dinner, when the sun goes down, we think of all that has happened this day. We come together, turn to God and say thanks. And we ask God to stay with us throughout the night, to forgive us for the things that we did wrong or the good things that we did not do during the day.

At Evening Prayer we usually sing Psalm 141: Our prayers rise like incense! And we also sing Mary's song of praise: "My soul proclaims the greatness of God, my spirit rejoices in God my Savior!" This is the song that Mary sang when she went to visit her cousin, Elizabeth. Elizabeth was waiting for John the Baptist to be born. Mary was waiting for Jesus to be born. Elizabeth told Mary that it was great that she was going to be the mother of Jesus, and Mary sang this song. The name of Mary's song in Latin is the *Magnificat* (mog-NI-fi-cot).

At Evening Prayer we might carry the paschal candle in and light everybody's candles from it—just like at the Easter Vigil. We might use incense during Psalm 141 and during Mary's song. The servers will help with this, and hold the book for the presider, too.

How Many Servers?

Either one, two or three servers will serve Morning or Evening Prayer. We'll name the servers for daily prayer Thurifer and Book. If a third server is used, Server 3 carries in the cross (just like at Mass) or the Easter candle (at vespers) at the beginning. Server 3 will not have to carry anything out, though. Daily prayer usually ends with a sign of peace and there is no final procession.

Thurifer at Morning Prayer

 There may be a procession of ministers in for Morning Prayer. Or the ministers may simply go to their seats and not have a procession in. Your leader will tell you.

If there is a procession, you'll carry the thurible and boat, just like at the beginning of Mass. You'll bow to the altar, put the thurible and boat on their stand and take your place.

If there is going to be a rite of blessing and sprinkling of holy water, go the presider. You will carry the bucket of water as the presider passes through the assembly to sprinkle everyone with the water of baptism at the start of this day.

At your seat, do what the rest of the assembly does: Sing the psalms, pay attention to the prayers and reading and preaching, sit and stand up tall.

After the reading and preaching (if there is preaching), there will be silence. After the silence, the presider will stand. All will begin to sing Zechariah's song, the Benedictus.

Fold your hands. Go to the thurible stand with Book. Take the thurible and the boat to the presider. (Book walks along with you.) Give the presider the boat and lift the thurible so the presider can put some incense in it. Then take the boat back and give the presider the thurible. The presider will incense the altar and the people. Go put the boat down. Fold your hands. Go back to the presider's chair. Stay there with your hands folded.

When the presider is done, take the thurible. Stand back a few feet. Bow, and incense the presider by swinging the thurible three times. Bow again. Go and put the thurible back on its stand. Fold your hands. Go to your seat. Do what the assembly does for the rest of the prayer.

There may be a procession out, just like at Mass. Or Morning Prayer may end with the sign of peace and people leaving. Make sure to share a sign of peace with people before cleaning up.

Thurifer at Evening Prayer

 There may be a procession of ministers in for Evening Prayer. Or the ministers may simply go to their seats and not have a procession in. Your leader will tell you.

When there is a procession for Evening Prayer, the procession goes to the Easter candle stand. Hand the presider the boat and lift up the thurible so the presider can put incense into the thurible. Then take the boat back and give the presider the thurible. After the presider incenses the candle and hands the thurible back to you, wait with the other ministers. The candle light will be shared, and a prayer of thanks for the light will be sung. When all the ministers go to their places, go and put the thurible on its stand. Stay there by it.

When all the ministers are at their places, Psalm 141 will begin. Add a little incense to the coal, and then go to

your seat. At your seat, do what the rest of the assembly does. Pick up your hymnal or song sheet and sing the psalms, listen to the reading and preaching, stand and sit with attention.

After the reading and preaching (if there is preaching), there will be silence. After the silence, the presider will stand. Everyone will begin singing Mary's song, the Magnificat.

Fold your hands. Go to the thurible stand with Book. Take the thurible and the boat to the presider. (Book walks along with you.) Give the presider the boat and lift the thurible just like before. Then take the boat back and give the presider the thurible. The presider will incense the altar and the people. Go put the boat down. Fold your hands. Go back to the presider's chair. Stay there with your hands folded.

When the presider is done, take the thurible. Stand back a few feet. Bow, and incense the presider by swinging the thurible three times. Bow again. Go and put the thurible back on its stand. Go to your seat. Do what the assembly does for the rest of the prayer.

There may be a procession out, just like at Mass. Or Evening Prayer may end with the sign of peace and people leaving. Make sure to share a sign of peace with people before cleaning up.

Holy Smoke!

Circle all the times that incense is used:

during the reading

during the singing of Psalm 141

during the singing of all psalms

during the singing of Mary's song

during the singing of Zechariah's song

at the Easter candle

when holy water is used

at the beginning

at the end

Book at Morning Prayer

 There may be a procession of ministers in for Morning Prayer. Or the ministers may simply go to their seats and not have a procession in. Your leader will tell you.

If there is a procession in, walk in with the ministers and bow to the altar just like at the beginning of Mass. The presider will carry the book, or it will be on the seat. So you will carry a hymnal or song sheet if a song is sung, or else fold your hands. Bow with the other ministers and take your place.

If there is going to be a rite of blessing and sprinkling of holy water, go the presider. Hold the book while the presider blesses the water. Then go to (or stay at) the presider's chair while the presider blesses everyone with the holy water of baptism at the start of the day. Hand the book to the presider when the presider returns to the chair, and go back to your seat.

At your seat, do what the rest of the assembly does. Pick up your hymnal or song sheet and sing the psalms, listen to the reading and the preaching, stand and sit with attention.

After each psalm, the presider will stand to say a prayer. Fold your hands. Go to the presider and hold the book. Give the book back to the presider at the end of the prayer. Fold your hands. Go back to your seat.

After the reading and preaching (if there is preaching), there will be silence. After the silence, the presider will stand. All will begin to sing Zechariah's song, the Benedictus.

Fold your hands. Go with Thurifer to the thurible stand. Then walk with Thurifer to the presider. Take the book from the presider and stand next to the presider's chair. Stay there until the presider returns.

If the presider needs the book for the prayers of the faithful, either hold the book open or hand the book to the presider. At the end of the petitions, hold the book open for the Lord's Prayer and for the final prayers and blessing. Then close the book. If there is a closing song, hand the book back to the presider. Otherwise, you may either carry it out or put it on the presider's chair.

Morning Prayer may end with the sign of peace and people leaving. Make sure to share a sign of peace with people before cleaning up.

Book at Evening Prayer

There may be a procession of ministers in for Evening Prayer. Or the ministers may simply go to their seats and not have a procession in. Your leader will tell you.

When there is a procession for Evening Prayer, the procession goes to the Easter candle stand. You may have to carry the book for the presider, if the presider carries the Easter candle. Otherwise, you may have a small candle. When the presider lights your candle, share the light with others. If you are not to hold a candle, you may have to hold the book open for the presider to sing a prayer of thanks for the light. Your leader will show you what to do.

When all the ministers go their seats, go to your place. At your seat, do what the rest of the assembly does. Pick up your hymnal or song sheet and sing the psalms, listen to the reading and preaching, stand and sit with attention.

After each psalm, the presider will stand to say a prayer. Fold your hands. Go to the presider and hold the book. Give the book back to the presider at the end of the prayer. Fold your hands. Go back to your seat.

After the reading and preaching (if there is preaching), there will be silence. After the silence, the presider will stand. All will begin to sing Zechariah's song, the Benedictus.

Fold your hands. Go with Thurifer to the thurible stand. Then walk with Thurifer to the presider. Take the book from the presider and stand next to the presider's chair. Stay there until the presider returns.

If the presider needs the book for the prayers of the faithful, either hold the book open or hand the book to the presider. At the end of the petitions, hold the book open for the Lord's Prayer and for the final prayers and blessing. Then close the book. If there is a closing song, hand the book back to the presider. Otherwise, you may either carry it out or put it on the presider's chair.

Evening Prayer may end with the sign of peace and people leaving. Make sure to share a sign of peace with people before cleaning up.

After Prayer

Don't forget to clean up. See page 6.
Don't forget these important things, even after prayer when you are cleaning up:

• Bow when you pass the altar.
• Genuflect when you pass the tabernacle.
• Carry things with both hands as if you are carrying eggs.
• Don't blow out the candles; use the extinguisher.
• Hang up your alb!

Serving at Devotions

Sunday Mass, daily Mass, daily prayer — these are the most important ways that we worship God together. But because God is so good, these are not the *only* ways that we worship God together. Everybody comes to Sunday Mass, and smaller groups of parishioners come at other times for **devotions**.

There are many kinds of devotions. Some devotions help us to remember and love the holy people who followed Jesus and who now pray for us to God, people like Saint Anthony or Saint Jude Thaddeus.

Many devotions help us to remember and love the Mother of God, Mary. Mary, too, prays for us. Some devotions help us to meditate on what Jesus did for us. The Stations of the Cross help us to walk the way of the cross that Jesus walked, so that we can be like him. Some devotions help us to remember and love Christ present in the tabernacle of the holy bread of life, the eucharist. These devotions are called Eucharistic Devotions or Devotion to the Blessed Sacrament.

Not every parish has all kinds of devotions. But if your parish has devotions, you may be asked to serve at them. Some devotions are celebrated on a certain day of the week, every week of the year. Others are celebrated only at special times, like Stations of the Cross in Lent or crowning the statue of Holy Mary in spring.

If you are asked to serve at a devotion, accept cheerfully. Come to church early as you would for Mass. Vest as you would for Mass. There may be some setting up to do — not like for Mass, but your leader will show you.

Three or two servers will be enough for most devotions. But if there is a special procession, maybe all the servers will be invited.

Here are some notes for serving two kinds of devotions: Stations of the Cross and Benediction of the Blessed Sacrament.

Serving at Stations of the Cross

 It's best if three servers serve at Stations. One carries the cross. Two carry candles.

 Serving Stations is easy. Have you seen the stations of the cross hanging on the walls surrounding the assembly in church? We walk from station to station. At each station, we stop to remember all that happened as Jesus died to save us. Prayers are said, and we sing and move on to the next station. The stations are like a parade!

Stations sometimes start in front of the altar and then move to station 1. Cross leads the procession into the assembly. Candle 1 and Candle 2 walk beside or behind Cross. Go to the altar

Here's a list of some devotions and blank spots for other devotions you parish might have. Find out which ones your parish has and write down when:

Devotion	When?
Prayers to St. Anthony	....
Prayers to St. Jude Thaddeus	....
(Write down devotions to other saints below:)	
....	....
....	....
....	....
Prayers to Our Mother of Perpetual Help	....
May Crowning	....
(Write down other devotions to Mary below:)	
....	....
....	....
Stations of the Cross	....
Benediction of the Blessed Sacrament	....
(Write down other devotions to Jesus below:)	
....	....
....	....

first. You may bow your head, but since you are holding something, don't bow your body and don't tip the cross or candle.

Usually, singing means it's time to move to the next station. If not, your leader will tell you what your signal is. Walk slowly. Cross should lead. But if the aisle is too narrow, Candle 1 may go first, followed by Cross, followed by Candle 2. At each station, you may bow your head, but since you are holding something, don't bow your body and don't tip the cross or candle.

There are 14 stations of the cross. At each one, listen carefully to the prayers that are said and the readings from scripture that might be used.

Often, Stations ends at the altar. The altar is sort of like a 15th station. If so, line up in front of the altar just as you did at the beginning.

When Stations is complete, if there is a liturgy of the word and preaching or something else, you will put the cross and candles in their stands and go to your place. Otherwise, you return to the sacristy.

If Stations is held in Lent, maybe you'll be lucky. Maybe the parish has a fish fry after, and you can go!

Benediction means "blessing." This devotion is a time to remember what we celebrate at Mass, and to remember that Christ is always present to us under the sign of bread in the tabernacle. (That's why the candle is always burning by the tabernacle.)

It's best if three servers serve Benediction, but two can do it. Server 1 carries the cross and holds the book. Server 2 handles the incense. Server 3 helps with the vessel for showing the host (the monstrance) and the special vestment, the humeral veil. Servers 1 and 3 also carry candles.

Before the devotion, prepare incense, processional candles in their place in the church the monstrance and the humeral veil.

Benediction happens in different ways. Your leader will show you how it is celebrated in your parish.

You will probably enter in procession and bow to the altar. Then you will take your places. Server 1 brings the book to the presider for the opening prayer and holds it. At your seat, do what the assembly does: Sing the songs, listen to the readings and preaching.

After the preaching, there may be some silence. After the silence, the presider will stand. If the monstrance is not already on the altar, Server 3 carries it there with two hands. Then Server 3 brings the humeral veil to the presider, who puts it on. Server 2

adds incense to the thurible and brings the boat. Server 1 gets both processional candles, and gives one to Server 3. With Server 2 going first with the thurifer and Servers 1 and 3 after, you lead the presider to the tabernacle. The presider will take the holy bread of the eucharist out of the tabernacle. Lead the presider back to the altar.

Line up in front of the altar. The presider will place the holy bread of the eucharist in the monstrance, then come around front. Servers 1 and 3 go and put their candles in their places. With hands folded, they return to the front of the altar. Server 2 hands the presider the boat and lifts the thurible so the presider can put incense into it. Then Server 2 hands the thurible to the presider and takes the boat back. All kneel as the presider incenses the holy bread of the eucharist.

Hymns may be sung and prayers may be said. All may pray silently for a while. It might be that the holy bread of the eucharist is going to be left in the monstrance for some time. This is called "exposition." If so, when the presider is ready, all of you stand, genuflect and process out. Server 2 carries the thurible and boat, but Servers 1 and 3 do not carry anything. They walk with folded hands.

If the holy bread of the eucharist is to be taken back to the tabernacle, go with the presider just like before. At the tabernacle, Server 2, holding the thurible, bows. Servers 1 and 3, holding candles, bow their heads, but don't bow their bodies or tip the candles. If you are not holding anything, genuflect. Then all process to the sacristy.

Serving through the Seasons

What's your favorite day of the year? Maybe it's your birthday, with cake and candles and singing and presents. Or maybe it's Christmas, with the tree twinkling with colorful lights and shiny glass balls, and presents wrapped in bright paper and tied with ribbons. Maybe it's the last day of school, when you've washed off the top of your desk and stacked all the books on the shelves for next year. Or maybe it's the first day of school, when your new shoes squeak on the clean floors and your pencils and crayons and markers are brand new.

Write down your favorite day of the year here:

As time passes
the church gets excited:
Jesus promised
that he would come back
at the end of time.
So as the seasons change,
we look for Christ
to come again.

The church has a favorite day, too. Can you guess the church's favorite day of the week? Here are some hints:

- It is the day when God created light.

- It is the first day of the week.

- It is the day of the week when Jesus rose from the dead — the third day.

- It is the day of the week when the Holy Spirit came down from heaven like wind and fire.

- It is the day of the week when the whole church comes together for Mass.

- It is the day that lets us take a peek at heaven.

- It is the day the Bible calls "the Day of the Lord."

Can you guess the church's favorite day of the week? Write your guess here:

Now turn the page and see if you are right!

Did you guess Sunday? Sunday is the church's favorite day of the week! (If you guessed another day, turn back the page and cross out your guess and write "Sunday" instead.)

To read more about the church's favorite day, see page 11. And you learned about serving Mass on Sunday on pages 43–49.

Sunday is the church's favorite day of the week. And every week of the year, we have Sunday to gather and to celebrate.

When the times of the year, the seasons, change, we know that we are growing up. Next summer you will be taller than you were last summer! And next fall, you will be in the next grade at school (if you study hard and do your homework!).

Sunday by Sunday, the seasons of the year unfold. And as time passes the church gets excited: Jesus promised that he would come back at the end of time. So as the seasons change, we look for Christ to come again. Not as a baby this time: Christ will come in glory and all the bad things that happen to people will stop. That's why we sing at Mass: "Christ has died. Christ is risen. *Christ will come again.*"

> Because Easter celebrates Christ's rising from the dead, it is our most holy celebration.

Seasons of the Year

So the church arranges Sundays in seasons, just like nature arranges our days into winter, spring, summer and fall. Some parts of the liturgy that we celebrate on Sunday never change. But other parts — like the entrance procession, the other rites for beginning, and which parts of the Bible we read and what prayers we say — do change. They change with the seasons. Sometimes these changes mean that the servers do things a little bit differently. So here's a quick look at the seasons of the church's year.

The Three Days

Just as Sunday is the church's favorite day of the week, Easter is the church's favorite day of the year. Because Easter celebrates Christ's rising from the dead, it is our most holy celebration. It is so important that it lasts for three days!

The Latin word **Triduum** is said like this: TRIH-doo-um. It means "the three days." The three days are these:

- from sunset Holy Thursday to sunset Good Friday
- from sunset Good Friday to sunset Holy Saturday
- from sunset Holy Saturday to sunset Easter Sunday.

In church, a day doesn't always start with morning. Sometimes it starts the night before when the sun goes down! Strange, isn't it? But it's an old

> Like Christ,
> like us,
> the baptized
> rise from the dead,
> rise from sin and sorrow
> and now live for God
> with us
> as sisters and brothers.
> This is
> so wonderful!

custom from long ago and far away. (That's why we can go to Sunday Mass on Saturday evening. When the sun goes down on Saturday, Sunday begins!)

The Triduum is our most important season. The church gathers together on each of the three days. We do amazing and fun things: We use lots of incense, we march (and march and march) in processions, we wash each other's feet, we kiss the cross, we light a bonfire, we light candles till the room glows, we hear lots and lots of stories about the wonderful things that God has done for us. Then we help God do the same things for people now: We baptize people in the water of the font, we pour expensive and sweet-smelling oil on their heads and rub it in, we give them a new robe to wear and a candle to light. Then we take them to the altar, the Lord's table, and share the body and the blood of Christ with them. Like Christ, like us, they rise from the dead, rise from sin and sorrow and now live for God with us as sisters and brothers. This is so wonderful!

More servers will be needed for the Triduum than for any other time of year. At this time of year more than any other, we have to make sure that our albs are clean and that all the vessels and other items in the church are polished and looking their best. If you are asked to serve during the Triduum, it is a great honor. You will have to come to church for practice because we will do special things. Listen carefully to what you are told, practice well and come to church early. Stay calm so that you can enjoy these beautiful liturgies. And even if you aren't serving all three days, come for all three days!

At home, try to turn off the TV and the computer games on Friday and Saturday. Give up pop and candy — even gum! Save your appetite for Easter's chocolate bunnies.

The Forty Days of Lent

Because the Triduum is so special, we have to get ready for it! The period of getting ready for the Triduum is called **Lent**, an old word that means "lengthen." During Lent, the hours of daylight get longer. Lent is springtime in the church!

Lent begins on Ash Wednesday, when we wear ashes on our forehead to show that we are made of earth and that God is our breath. Lent is the time when the people who will be baptized make their final preparations. And we who are already baptized help them by doing works of **penance**.

Works of penance help us to be sorry for the bad things that we have done: the lies we might have told, the fights we might have had and things like that. Penance also helps us to be sorry for the bad things that happen in the world: when people who are different from each other don't get along, when poor people sleep outside because there is no room for them, when children go to bed hungry because governments and people don't care and share. These things are not our fault, but we are still sorry that they happen! And with Christ leading us, we want to change these things. Works of penance help us to change and be more like Christ each day.

What are the works of penance that we can do in Lent? There are too many to list! But the church has three kinds of good things to do:

- Pray

- Fast (give up some things we like)

- Share what we have with the poor.

During Lent, the church prays more. In addition to Sunday Mass and daily Mass, the parish might have Morning or Evening Prayer (see pages 62–66), or Stations of the Cross (see pages 67–70) or some other devotions. You may be asked to serve at these prayer times. Even if you have to get up early or go to church after school, serve cheerfully. And even if you aren't scheduled to serve, check out these different kinds of prayer!

Grown-ups **fast** during Lent: They eat less food, or maybe on some days, no food at all. Because you are still growing and you need your nourishment, maybe you shouldn't fast like that. But you can stop eating things that you don't need: candy, dessert or popcorn when you watch TV. And when you give these things up, you can say a quiet prayer like this:

> God, Jesus gave up his life
> so that we may live.
> I give up (here say what you are giving up)
> so that I may be more like Jesus.
> Some people go without food
>   not by choice,
> but because they have none.
> Help them find enough to eat
>   this day.

During Lent, we try to share more of what we have with people who are in need. Maybe at school or religious education class you are given a cardboard bank shaped like a rice bowl, or a plastic bank shaped like a loaf of bread. Can you put some of your allowance in it? Maybe you can clean up your neighborhood by picking up cans and bottles, and then cash them in and put that money in this bank. Then at the

> Lent is the time
> when
> the people who will be baptized
> make their final preparations.
> And we who are already baptized
> help them
> by doing works of penance.

end of Lent, the church collects the money and shares it with the needy. This is called "giving alms" and **almsgiving** is an important part of Lent. It teaches us how to share what we have on all the other days of the year, too!

Sunday Mass in the beginning of Lent is pretty much the same as ever, except that the vestments will be purple, and we will not sing our happiest and holiest song, "Alleluia!" We may use incense. On the third, fourth and fifth Sundays of Lent, the people who will be baptized come forward for special prayers. A server may have to hold the book for the presider, but that's not hard! The last Sunday of Lent is Palm Sunday of the Passion of the Lord. That's the time when we remember when Jesus went to Jerusalem for the last time before he died on the cross. The people welcomed him by waving palm branches and putting them on the road for his donkey to walk on. At church, we are all given palm branches, and we walk in procession so we can follow Jesus better. The gospel will be very long this day, and the servers will not hold candles or carry incense. But listen to the gospel carefully: This is the story of how Jesus died so that we might live with God.

The Fifty Days of Easter

We spend the 40 days of Lent getting ready for the 3 days, the Triduum. Then we have 50 days to celebrate! The season of Easter begins on Easter Sunday and lasts until Pentecost Sunday. So make sure that you save some jelly beans from your Easter basket. Don't eat them all on Sunday morning!

The **Easter season** is our happiest time of year. We put flowers all over the church, and outside, the crocuses and tulips and daffodils begin to poke through the slushy ground. They grow and grow and grow until they bloom — beautiful colors and sweet smells. The leaves come back to the trees and crickets come out of hiding. We look for robins and maybe even see blue robin eggs in a nest! We put away our winter clothes and wear our spring jackets. We even get to leave our boots at home and run around in our shoes again!

The Easter season
is our happiest time of year.
We put flowers
all over the church,
and outside,
the crocuses and tulips and
daffodils begin to poke
through
the slushy ground.

For servers, Sunday Mass does not change much during the Easter season, but listen for the Alleluias in our songs, and sing out! We may use incense every Sunday. The vestments are white until Pentecost. Then they are red. At the beginning of Mass, the presider may sprinkle the holy water of baptism on all the people. You may have to help with that by carrying the bucket. And maybe the processional cross that you carry is all decorated with flowers and ribbons and things. Before Mass, practice holding it right if it is decorated. Servers may also carry banners on poles in the processions, but your leader will let you know.

Ordinary Time lasts all summer long and through the fall, too.

Ordinary Time

After Pentecost, we count off the Sundays until the end of the year. We number each Sunday so that we can number the scripture readings in the lectionary and the prayers in *The Roman Missal* . That way, we can go through them one by one and not forget any! This time of year is called "ordinary." *Ordinary* here does not mean "not special" or "boring." It means something else.

Remember in math class when you learned about numbers? Remember the "ordinal" numbers: 1st, 2nd, 3rd, 4th, and so on? These are the numbers that we use to count things. If you haven't already, later you will learn in school about other kinds of numbers: negative numbers and Roman numerals and other such things. In the church, **Ordinary Time** is the time of counted Sundays. But don't worry: You don't have to remember these numbers!

Sunday Mass during Ordinary Time is Sunday Mass as it is always celebrated. The vestments are green. Ordinary Time lasts all summer long and through the fall, too. The few weeks between Christmas and Lent are the beginning of Ordinary Time. But then Lent and Easter interrupt.

During Ordinary Time in the summer and fall, you will serve wedding Masses on Friday evenings and Saturdays. And there will be holy days that are not on Sundays but will feel like Sunday: The whole church will gather and even though it is a Tuesday or a Thursday, a Wednesday or a Friday, Mass will be like Sunday Mass!

During summer it may be hard to come to church to serve, especially if you have to serve daily Mass when you would rather be running through the sprinkler or playing baseball. But be a faithful server. And don't wear your bathing suit to church!

Finally, it will be fall, and school will start. Then Halloween will come, and the next day we celebrate All Saints — a holy day. Then at church we will remember all the people that we love who have died — on All Souls Day and all through November.

Advent

When the last days of Ordinary Time in November are done, the new church year begins. January 1 is New Year's Day for the world, but in church, new year's day is a month or so earlier, on the First Sunday of Advent. The season of Advent is made up of the weeks before Christmas.

Sunday Mass during Advent is not much different than other times. The beginning may be changed a little. During Advent, we light the candles on the Advent wreath. A server may light the candles, or someone else will. You may have to carry the incense for the presider to incense the wreath. Your leader will tell you.

The Advent wreath is like a clock. It helps us keep track of the hours that lead up to Christmas. It is also like a crown. In the old days, when the Olympics began in Greece, athletes who won a contest were given a wreath to wear on their heads. It was made from the green branches of the laurel tree. (When your mom or dad makes a pot of chili in the winter, does a dried bay leaf go into the pot? The bay leaf is from the same kind of tree that the athletes' laurel wreaths came from!) The Advent wreath, made of the green branches of an evergreen tree, is a winner's crown, too. It is a crown for Christ and for us, the Body of Christ. The race is done, the prize is won: Christ beat death and rose again on the third day forever. Each week in Advent, we light one more candle, and at the end of the four Sundays, the fiery crown is ready and we hope that Christ comes again in glory very soon.

Christmas

And we know that Christ will come again in glory at the end of time. How? Because he came the first time, just as God promised. God promised that the Savior would come, and in Bethlehem, Jesus was born to Mary and Joseph.

We remember Christ's first coming, Christ's birth, in the great festival of **Christmas**. Second to Easter, Christmas is the church's favorite time of year! It's more than just Jesus' birthday. It is that, and more.

At Christmas, we remember that Christ was born and laid in a manger. What is a manger? It is a food dish for animals! The baby who lies in the manger will grow up and say, "I am the bread of life. If you eat this bread and drink this cup you will live with me forever."

At Christmas, we remember that the poor shepherds saw God and adored, while the kings and princes tried to kill the baby. We remember that the magi, those strange foreigners, also saw that Jesus was the Savior. This is the great feast of Epiphany. And the church gets excited on this day because we were once outsiders ourselves, but Jesus has welcomed us into God's reign.

We remember that when he was grown up, Jesus was baptized by John in the River Jordan. We, too, are baptized, and so we must live as Jesus lived. And during the holy Christmas season, we remember that Jesus went to a wedding

> The Christmas season
> is like
> the church's wedding party.
> When Jesus came,
> heaven married earth.
> And plain old water tasted
> as good as the best wine —
> or soda,
> if you like that better!

in the town of Cana. When the wine ran out, and the bride and groom were afraid that the guests would have nothing more to drink and that the party would end, Jesus turned water into wine. The waiter in charge said it was wonderful wine! And the party continued.

The Christmas season is like the church's wedding party. When Jesus came, heaven married earth. And plain old water tasted as good as the best wine—or soda, if you like that better!

At home and in church, we set up the Christmas tree and decorate it with lights and ornaments and all kinds of fun things. When you look at the Christmas tree, think of the cross. The cross was made from a tree. And Jesus was killed by being nailed to the cross. But Jesus rose from the dead because love is stronger than hate, stronger even than death. By rising from the dead, Jesus turned the cross into the tree of life. The shining Christmas tree reminds us of the tree of life.

Sunday Mass during the Christmas season doesn't change. But on Christmas Eve, there may be two or three Masses and some things will be a little different. At the Christmas midnight Mass, the opening procession will be special. Incense will probably be used, too. And there may be one or two more servers than usual. But your leader will explain everything for you.

There Is a Season

The Bible says, "There is a season for everything, a time for every purpose under heaven." In the church, we have a season for everything, special times and days that help us remember Jesus and all that he did and said. More importantly, the different seasons help us to spend time with Jesus now, to be more like Jesus now. As time passes, we not only grow older and taller and smarter, we grow into Christ!

What's your favorite season of the **church's year**? Is it Advent with its wreath? Christmas with its tree? Lent with its ashes? Easter with the newly baptized, with the fire and water and oil? Ordinary Time when we count the days?

Write down your favorite time of the church year below:

```
..........................................................................................
```

Make Your Own Church Calendar

On the next page is a circle that shows all the seasons of the church's year. It is divided into slices, like a big ring-shaped cake. Each week is one slice, with Sunday on the outside and Saturday on the inside. Look up the date of Easter Sunday for next year and write it in the square just below the word Triduum. Color the three days of the Triduum with a yellow or gold marker or crayon. Find the section marked Christmastime. It starts on December 25, goes twelve days and then to the next Sunday. Color all these days with a yellow or gold crayon or marker.

The section before Christmas covers four Sundays. Color all these days purple for Advent. The section before Triduum covers six Sundays and then four more days to Ash Wednesday. Color all these days purple for Lent. The section marked Eastertime covers seven Sundays. Color these days a bright favorite color! Leave the next two Sundays white, but color all of the other days in the calendar green. Now you have a colorful church calendar!

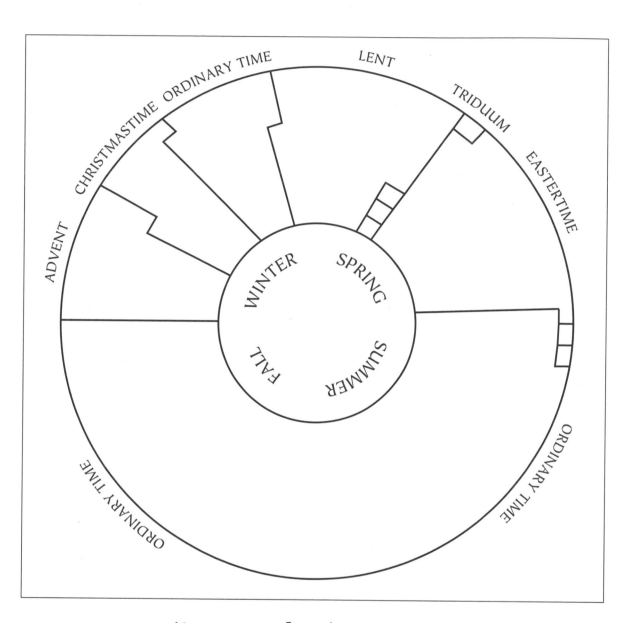

Write the date of Easter Sunday in the square.
Color the Triduum section gold or yellow.
Color the Christmastime section gold or yellow.
Color the Advent section purple.
Color the Lent section purple.
Color the Eastertime section with your favorite bright color.
Leave the next two Sundays white.
Color the Ordinary Time sections green.

Serving when the Bishop Comes

Who is the **bishop**? Why does the bishop come to visit us in our parish?

Do you know what a shepherd is? What a shepherd does? A shepherd takes care of a whole bunch of sheep. Feeding them. Guarding them. Guiding them. Jesus is our Good Shepherd.

After Jesus died on the cross and rose from the dead, he ascended into heaven. But he did not leave us orphans. He sent the Holy Spirit, first on the apostles and then on all his followers. He told his apostles to be like shepherds for all who are baptized.

The bishops are leaders who are shepherds for the church, like the apostles who lived long ago. That's why the bishop carries a shepherd's staff, called a **crosier**.

You know your **pastor**. Your pastor is the priest who takes care of your parish. (The word *pastor* is a Latin word that means shepherd, someone who takes care of sheep.) Well, the bishop is the pastor of all the parishes in the area called the **diocese**. If the diocese is large or special, it's called an **archdiocese**. Then the bishop is called an **archbishop**.

Write down the name of your parish here:

```
_____
```

Now write down the name of the diocese that your parish is in:

```
_____
```

Now write down the name of your bishop:

```
_____
```

If you listen carefully, at every Mass in the great eucharistic prayer, you'll hear that we pray that God will guide the bishop of Rome, who is also the **pope**.

Now write down the name of the bishop of Rome, the pope:

```
_____
```

After hearing the name of the pope in the great eucharistic prayer, you will then hear the name of your own bishop. At this time we pray for our own bishop by name.

Why the Bishop Comes

The bishop comes to our parish out of love and concern for us. Sometimes, the bishop comes just for a visit! More often, the bishop comes for a particular reason: to preside over the celebration of confirmation, usually once a year or so. Or the bishop will come for the funeral if one of the priests dies. And if we build a new church, or fix up the old one, the bishop will come for that celebration, too.

New deacons and priests are usually ordained at the bishop's church, the **cathedral**. But sometimes the bishop comes to the parish church for this celebration.

When the bishop comes, no matter what day of the week it is, it is like Sunday for us! If the bishop comes just for a visit, four servers will be scheduled. Serve just like on Sunday.

  When the bishop comes for confirmation or to dedicate the church building, two more servers will be assigned. These two servers have a special job: One takes care of the bishop's staff (the crosier) and another takes care of the bishop's pointy hat (the **miter**).

 Taking care of the bishop's miter and crosier is pretty easy. The bishop's secretary will tell you what to do. You may be given a cape to wear. It's called a humeral veil because it goes around your shoulders. (The word *humeral* comes from a Latin word that means "shoulder." The long bone in your upper arm, the one that goes from your shoulder to your elbow, is called your "humerus." So Latin words show up in other places besides church!) The humeral veil goes around your shoulders and is fastened either with ties or with clasps in the front.

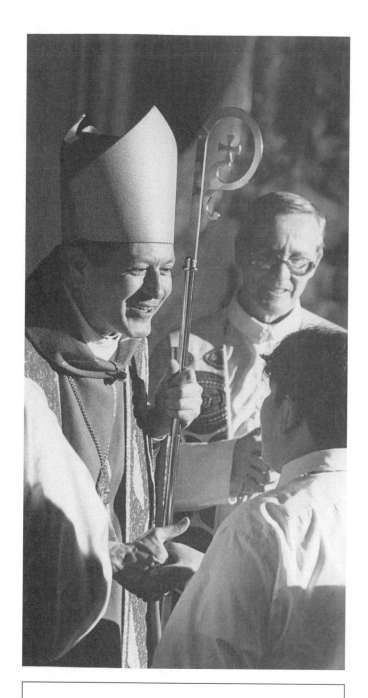

The bishops
are shepherds for the church,
like the apostles
who lived long ago.
That's why the bishop carries
a shepherd's staff.

Your hands slip into the hems of the veil like gloves. With your hands in the veil, you hold the crosier or the miter whenever the bishop doesn't need them.

At the beginning of the liturgy, the two extra servers walk in behind the bishop. After you bow to the altar, you step aside — out of the way, but near enough for the bishop's secretary or your pastor to hand you the crosier or miter. Just keep your eye on the bishop's secretary (or your pastor, if the bishop doesn't have a secretary).

When you hold the crosier or miter, hold it carefully and don't fuss with it. When you are not holding the crosier or miter, don't play with the humeral veil, either. Fold your hands outside of the veil when you are not holding the crosier or miter with it.

At all times, make sure that you do what the assembly does: Pay attention, sing, make the responses, sit, stand, bow, kneel and the like.

> When the bishop comes, no matter what day of the week it is, it is like Sunday for us!

Two Extra Jobs

Whenever the bishop uses the holy oil, Candle 1 and Candle 2 have an extra job. When the anointing is almost over, the bishop's secretary (or your pastor) will signal for you. Candle 1 will bring the water pitcher and bowl. Candle 2 will bring the towel and a plate with a few slices of lemon on it. Come forward, but wait off to the side.

After the bishop anoints people or the altar with the holy oil of chrism, the bishop's secretary (or your pastor) will signal you to come forward. Candle 2 offers the bishop the slices of lemon — lemon juice helps wash off the sticky oil. After the bishop squeezes the lemon slices and puts them back on the plate, Candle 1 places the bowl under the bishop's hands and pours water over them — just like at Mass. Candle 2 then offers the towel.

One thing is different: The bishop will be sitting on the chair. If the chair is too high up, you may have to kneel on the step to help with the hand-washing.

After this hand-washing, the Mass will proceed. And you do all the things that you'd do at a Sunday Mass. You might even have to help with the regular hand-washing, if the bishop does so at the usual time in the Mass. Just pay close attention to the bishop's secretary (or your pastor).

Wearing Baptism's Robe

When we go to different places, we wear different clothes: fancy clothes for parties, dress clothes for school and church, play clothes at home, uniforms for sports. What are your favorite kinds of clothes? Why are these your favorite?

In the house of the church, baptized people can wear very special clothes: the robe of baptism. When you were baptized, after you were bathed in the font's water and rubbed with the holy oil called chrism, you were dressed in a white garment. The minister said these words to you, calling you by name:

> You have become a new creation, and have clothed yourself in Christ. See in this white garment the outward sign of your Christian dignity. With your family and friends to help you by word and example, bring that dignity unstained into the everlasting life of heaven.

This makes sense: What do you do after you take a bath? You get dressed! But the clothes that were put on you after baptism were more than just plain old clothes. They were a sign that now you belong to a bigger family, the family of God.

The Bible says that at the end of the world, the people who serve God will wear bright new clothes and shine like the sun. They will stand around God's throne and see Jesus, the Lamb of God. Listen to the dream that John had, written down in the Bible's last book, the Book of Revelation:

I saw a large crowd with more people than could be counted. They were from every race, tribe, nation, and language, and they stood before the throne and the Lamb. They wore white robes. . . . The angels who stood around the throne kneeled in front of it with their faces to the ground. . . . They all worshipped God and said, "Amen! Praise, glory, wisdom, thanks, honor, power, and strength belong to our God forever and ever. Amen!" One of the elders asked me, "Do you know who these people are that are dressed in white robes? Do you know where they come from?"

Can you answer the elder's question? Who are all the people dressed in the white robes? Write your answer here:

....
....

Read on to see if you are right:

"Sir," I answered, "you must know." Then he told me: "These are the ones who have gone through the great suffering. They have washed their robes in the blood of the Lamb and have made them white. And so they stand before the throne of God and worship God in the temple day and night. The one who sits on the throne will spread his tent over them. They will never hunger or thirst again, and they won't be troubled by the sun or any scorching heat. The Lamb in the center of the throne will be their shepherd. He will lead them to streams of life-giving water, and God will wipe all tears from their eyes."

We can be the people wearing the robes in the Bible's dream! We can be the people who stand at God's altar, giving thanks and praise! We are the people that Jesus leads to life-giving water: the water of baptism. We are the people who wear baptism's robe!

Ask your mom or dad if they still have your baptismal garment. Can you see it? It probably won't fit you now! If they don't have the garment, maybe they have a picture of you in it! Ask to see the picture.

When you join a sports team or become Boy Scout or a Girl Scout, you are given a uniform. When you wear that uniform, you know that you belong. And everybody sees that you are a member of the team. When you wear baptism's robe, know that you belong to the church. Be happy that you are a child of God, and that Jesus is your brother.

Since your baptismal garment probably doesn't fit you any more, the church has lots of them in the sacristy for everybody to share.

When it is worn at liturgy, baptism's robe is called an **alb**, from a Latin word meaning "white." Anyone who is baptized could wear an alb, but usually only some of the ministers of the liturgy do. As a server, you wear an alb. And the bishop, priest and deacon all wear albs underneath the other vestments that they wear. Before they put on the vestments of their ministry, they first put on baptism's robe.

Find an alb that fits you well. Try it on. The end of it shouldn't touch the floor or make you trip. But it should cover your legs!

Always put your alb on and take it off carefully. Always remember to hang it up after Mass. Handle and wear the alb with respect. It is a sign of holy baptism. When we wear it, we are wrapping ourselves in God's love. When we take it off and hang it up, we are promising God that we will share God's love with other people and be good. And then when it is time to serve God with gladness another time, we will again put on our uniform, baptism's robe.

Lighting Candles

Think about your birthday. Remember sitting in the dark waiting for the cake to be carried in, all lit up with candles? Maybe the cake was already on the table, and then someone turned off the lights. Remember when your mom or dad or big sister or big brother lit the match? The candle flames dance and shine like stars in the night sky. Maybe you had trick candles: candles that lit up again after you blew them out!

When you were baptized, after you were bathed in the font and anointed with chrism, the parish gave you two gifts. One was a new robe, your baptismal garment. The other was a candle. We lit your candle from the big Easter candle. Your godfather or godmother held the candle for you. The presider said to you, "Receive the light of Christ." Then the presider told everybody that Jesus shines on you, in you. Now you must walk as a child of the light.

Every time we hold a lighted candle, we remember our baptism. We remember that Jesus shines on us like the sun and that love is like a flame in our hearts. We remember that we must shine the light of love on others, be the light of love so that others know the way to Jesus.

How can you shine the light of love for others? Write down two things you can do to help others:

1...

....

2...

....

At Mass, you'll carry candles in procession to show our love for the holy cross. You'll carry candles next to the holy book of the readings, to show our love for God's word. You might even hold the candles, standing straight and tall next to the ambo, as the holy scriptures are proclaimed. Sometimes you may lead the people who bring up the gifts of bread and wine

by carrying candles before them, showing them the way to the altar.

Before Mass you will light candles and after Mass you will put them out. (Or maybe this is the sacristan's job.) When you light the candles near the ambo or when you carry the candles next to the book, remember this: In the beginning of time, before anything was made, God said, "Let there be light," and there was light. When you light the candles near the altar, or carry candles to lead people with their gifts, remember this: Jesus said, "I am the light of the world. Come to me and you will have the light of life." When you light the candles to walk next to the cross, say this prayer to God: "Your word is a lamp for my steps, a light for my path." When you light the big Easter candle for funerals or during Eastertime, remember this: Christ is risen from the dead!

To light the candles, hold the candle pole with two hands. Adjust the wick so that the flame is not too big, but so that it doesn't go out. Gently touch the flame to the candle's wick. Hold it there until the candle is lit.

When you put out the candles, gently put the extinguisher cup over the flame. Wait until the flame goes out. But don't touch the top of the candle or the metal or glass cap with the extinguisher. (The melted wax will spill!) Never blow a candle out in church. It'll make a mess!

Whenever you carry a candle, hold your arms away from your body and keep the candle pointed up straight. Don't tip it. Don't breathe on the flame or it might go out. If your candle goes out while you are walking in procession, leave it. Later, if you have a chance to light it again without making a fuss, do so. Don't tip a burning candle (or one that's just gone out to light it): Wax will spill.

The candles on your birthday cake, the candle that was given to you on your baptism day, the candles on your dining room table, the candles around our altar — all these remind us that Jesus is our light and love is like a flame. When we light a candle, let's think of Jesus. And even though we have to put the candles out when our prayer is done, let's promise to walk always like children of the light and to keep the flame of love alive in our hearts.

Carrying the Cross

Make the sign of the cross on your body: Touch your forehead, then your stomach, then your left shoulder and then your right. Why do we do this every day of our lives?

Do you remember the first time that the sign of the cross was made on you? Probably not! When a baby is born and brought to the church, we make the sign of the cross on the little one's forehead. We say: "You now belong to Christ." Then we baptize the baby and welcome him or her into our family: the people who belong to Christ, the people who are marked with the sign of the cross.

From that day on, every day of our lives, before and after every meal we eat and every prayer we say, before we get out of bed and before we fall asleep, we trace the sign of the cross on our bodies.

When we gather together to give God thanks and praise, we carry the cross into our assembly. We carry it high, so that everyone can see it. We carry it slowly and carefully, so that everyone can follow it. We set it up in our midst so that everyone can gather around it. When the cross is carried in and set up, we know that the church is gathered. And when the church is gathered, each person who is baptized makes the sign of that cross on his or her body. Then we are gathered in Christ's name. Then we know that Christ is here.

Carrying the cross in procession is a great honor. Many times a server carries the cross. But sometimes an usher or another baptized person will carry it — especially if it is big and heavy! The person who carries the cross is called the cross-bearer. Another name for the cross-bearer is crucifer. Sometimes we carry burning incense before the cross, swirling sweet-smelling clouds of smoke around it. Sometimes we carry candles next to the cross, because the cross is holy.

Remember the story of Simon of Cyrene? The soldiers had beat Jesus badly. He was weak and hurt. When they led him away to the hill to kill him, they made him carry the cross. When they reached the hill, they were going to nail him to it and hang him up. But he kept falling because he was weak and hurt. Then the soldiers saw Simon. Simon was visiting Jerusalem from another country. Maybe he was on vacation. Maybe he was buying or selling some things. Maybe he was just walking down the street minding his own business, wondering why all the people were crowded around, shouting.

The soldiers forced Simon to carry the cross for Jesus. Maybe Simon was angry and didn't want to do this. Or maybe Simon felt sorry for Jesus and hoped that he could help Jesus, even just a little. The story doesn't tell us.

But the story tells us that we should be like Simon of Cyrene. We should help Jesus carry the cross.

We remember what Jesus said to us before he was hung on the cross: "Take up your cross and follow me."

In Jesus' time, the cross was a horrible tool to hurt and kill people: criminals and poor people, people who were different, not liked or not understood. Today, nobody nails criminals or poor people, different people or strange people to wood crosses. But prejudice and poverty, injustice and hatred are all like crosses. On them we nail other people until they are dead. And when they suffer, Jesus suffers, too.

Look around your neighborhood. Look around your church, your school, your home. How are people who are poor or different or strange treated? Are they loved or are they hated? How are people treated who make mistakes or do bad things? Are they forgiven or are they punished too hard? Think of all these things when you see the cross.

Jesus turned a bad thing into a good thing. The cross was used to hurt and kill him — and many other poor people, too. But he rose from the dead and forgave everyone, loving us all. The dead wood of the cross became the living tree of life and love. Marked with this sign of the cross, this sign of Jesus, we too must turn bad things into good things.

We must carry the cross not only in church, when it is our turn to be the cross bearer, but also every day. We must look for the chance to be like Simon, to help other people carry the crosses that hurt them. We must share what we have with people who have nothing. We must stand up for people who are treated badly. We must visit people who are lonely and forgive people who hurt us. Then we are not only like Simon, helping others carry their crosses. Then we are like Jesus, who turned death into life.

Will you be like Simon of Cyrene? When you help others, you help Jesus. Will you help others carry their crosses? If so, then you are ready to carry the cross in church. Then you are ready to lift high the cross of Christ in the assembly of the baptized people, the people who follow Jesus, the people who are marked with the sign of the cross.

Think about these things before it is your turn to carry the holy cross in church. Write down two things that you can do to help other people who carry some kind of cross:

1...

2...

Holding the Book

Have you ever held a shopping bag for your dad so that he could unlock the door? Have you ever held one tool for your mom while she was using another one to fix something? Or maybe you held a friend's can of soda so that he or she could tie a shoe. These simple, small acts of kindness are good. We help each other in little ways and God is pleased.

In the liturgy, servers do small, kind acts that help the community pray better. Servers carry and hold many things that the assembly needs and uses to worship God, to give thanks and praise. One important thing that a server holds is the book of prayers, **The Roman Missal.** The server holds the book so that the presider can stand with outstretched arms and speak to God. The words that the presider says are words that we all are praying in our hearts.

Why does the presider stand this way: with arms stretched wide, hands open? What does it look like? Write down what you think it looks like, or draw a picture of the presider standing this way:

Does it look like Jesus on the cross? The presider stands with open arms to remind us that Jesus opened his arms wide to gather all people to God's breast, just like when your mom or grandmom hugs you, snuggling you safe. The presider stands with open hands to gather up all of our prayers and give them to God. And with open hands, the presider receives from God the answers to our prayers. It is important that the presider stand this way. And to help the presider do so, the server holds the book so that the presider can read and say the words. Sometimes the server holds the book so that the presider can do something

> Holding the book of prayers is a simple, kind act that helps the assembly give God thanks and praise better.

else: bless water or wedding rings, for example.

The two times that the server holds the book at Sunday Mass are for the opening prayer and for the prayer after communion. You might bring the book forward when the presider says, "Let us pray." Or maybe you will have to bring it before the presider says, "Let us pray." Your leader will explain. But when you carry the book to the presider, do it like this:

Make sure that the right ribbon book marker is sticking out of the middle of the side of the book, not the bottom. Hold the book with two hands by the two bottom corners, with the top of book resting against your chest. Make sure that the front cover faces out. Walk slowly, but not too slow. Walk carefully, but don't act stuffy! Stand in front of the presider. Be careful if there is a microphone stand. Stand up straight. Raise the book so that it is high enough for the presider to read. If you are tall enough, you will be able to leave the top of the book resting against your chest. If you are shorter (it's OK!), you may have to hold the book up higher, maybe in front of your face.

The presider may open the book as you hold it. Or you may have to open the book to the proper page. Your leader will tell you. If you open the book, hold the spine corner with one hand. Grab the ribbon marker with the other and carefully pull the book open. Slip your fingers in the open page so that the book won't flop shut. Open the book all the way. Then place each hand on the bottom corner of the open book. If the presider opens the book, slide your hands along the bottom so that each hand is on a bottom corner of the open book. Practice this many times before you begin serving.

When you hold the book, stand very still! Stand up tall! When the opening prayer is finished, either the presider will close the book or you will. After the prayer after communion, you may have to keep the book open for a final blessing. Or if announcements are made, you may have to bring the book back for the final blessing. The presider or your leader will tell you. After the book is closed, carry it back the same way that you carried it forward. Put it on the credence table or at your seat — whatever your leader tells you. Never set it on the floor. And don't sit on it!

At weddings and funerals, or when baptism is celebrated at Mass, you may have to carry the rite book in the procession to the door. Carry it like *The Roman Missal*: Hold the bottom corners. Let the top rest against your chest. Make sure that the front faces out.

Don't carry *The Roman Missal* or the baptism book, the wedding book or the funeral book high up over your head. We only carry the lectionary and

gospel book that way because those books hold the word of God.

Holding the book of the prayers is a simple, kind act that helps the assembly better give God thanks and praise. It's an honor to hold this holy book. For inside this book are the words that we say to God. Think about it. We talk to the God who made the sun and moon and stars, the God who helped the poor Hebrew slaves escape from Pharaoh's army, the God who became one of us in Jesus, the God who raised Jesus from the dead. To this great and powerful God, we say the simple words in this special book. And God hears us and answers us.

Burning Incense

Have you ever barbecued hamburgers and hot dogs? Roasted corn or vegetables on the grill? How about marshmallows? Did you notice how the smells fill the air? You know it's dinnertime when you smell food cooking!

You know it's Christmas when you smell pine trees. You know it's spring when you smell tulips and hyacinths. You know it's fall when you smell dead leaves. It's Halloween when you smell pumpkin guts as you carve the jack-o-lantern. And how do you know it's Thanksgiving Day?

Smells can tell us what time it is. In church, we burn incense when it's time to give God thanks and praise, and when it's time to ask God for help. And just as the sweet perfumed smoke rises to the ceiling, so do our prayers go to God's ears.

Incense comes from trees and other plants. The sticky stuff inside some trees and plants — called resin — hardens into chunks. The chunks don't smell very much. But when you put them on a burning coal, they melt. Then the beautiful smell comes out and fills the room.

The bowl that we burn incense in is called a **thurible**. Sometimes a thurible is a ceramic bowl filled with sand or pebbles. The sand or pebbles hold the heat from the burning coal and keep the bowl from breaking. Sometimes the thurible is a metal bowl on a chain. We can swing the bowl on the chain to make the incense burn faster and the smoke spread farther. The grains of incense are kept in a dish called a **boat**. The boat has a spoon. The server who carries the thurible is called the **thurifer**.

Look at the picture of the thurible at the bottom of this page. Add smoke to it. Draw the smoke by using the side of the pencil's tip (not its point). Hold the pencil like a fork, with the side of the tip pressed against the page. Then move your wrist back and forth up toward the top of the page. Add three or four wisps of smoke this way.

We burn incense in church to send our prayers to God and to smell God's goodness and love. So we burn incense and swirl the sweet smoke around holy people and holy things, and when we sing or say holy words.

We burn incense as we carry the holy cross in, wrapping the assembly of God's holy people in holy smoke. Then we know that Mass has begun! The presider wraps the altar in a cloud of

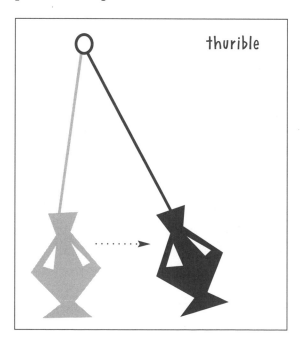

thurible

holy smoke, too. We remember that this table is where heaven meets earth. And just like the mountains have clouds of mist surrounding their tops, our altar has sweet clouds dancing around it, too.

We burn incense before the book of God's word, before we tell the stories and teachings of Jesus. And as we listen to the holy words with our ears, we smell the sweet smoke with our noses. We burn incense and send up a cloud of smoke over our altar, over our bread and wine. God's angel comes in the clouds of smoke and takes our bread and wine to heaven and brings the bread of life and the cup of salvation down for us.

And before the assembly of God's holy people offers the great prayer of praise and thanks, the deacon or a server incenses them. We wrap the assembly in holy smoke one last time just before the presider says, "Lift up your hearts." We wrap the baptized people in a cloud of holy smoke just before they say, "We lift them up to the Lord." So just as the smoke goes up to the ceiling and touches the sky, so will our hearts go to God. And just like our noses smell the sweet perfume of prayer, so we will smell that God is here. And then we know that heaven will smell good, like a new morning after a fresh rain, or like bread baking in the oven.

At Morning Prayer, we burn incense when we sing the song of Zechariah: "Blessed be the God of Israel!" We burn more incense when we offer up our prayers for help. At Evening Prayer we burn incense when we sing Psalm 141: "My prayers rise like incense." And we burn more when we sing Mary's song: "My soul magnifies God and my spirit rejoices in my savior!" And we keep it burning when we offer up our prayers for help.

At funerals, we show our love for the person who has died. We burn incense and wrap the coffin in a sweet cloud of smoke. We pray that just as the incense rises to the sky, so will this person who has died go to God.

At devotions, we burn incense to show our love for Jesus by wrapping the bread of the eucharist in clouds of holy smoke. And we honor Mary and the saints by burning incense before a statue or picture.

You will practice how to be the thurifer, how to serve God and God's people by making sweet clouds. But here are some things to remember:

If you are carrying a bowl thurible, hold it with both hands. Hold it away

from your body. Gently move it back and forth to send the smoke up.

If you are carrying a thurible on a chain in procession, let it swing gently at your side. Hold your arm out so that the thurible doesn't hit your leg when you walk. If you are not carrying the boat in the other hand, put your free hand over your heart.

The coal has to be red-hot to melt the incense. So light the coal about ten minutes before the liturgy begins. Don't hold the coal in your hand to light it. Use a pair of tongs to hold it up. Or use a wick instead of a match and touch the wick to the coal until it sparks. Then blow on it a little. Don't touch the coal after you've lit it. Even if it doesn't look red, it may still burn you.

When you put incense on the coal, tap the coal with the spoon when you pour the incense. When the priest or deacon is going to add the incense, hand over the boat and then lift up the thurible. If the thurible has a lid, you'll have to raise it. But use the chain or the wood knob. Don't touch the metal lid: It's hot!

When the priest or deacon adds the incense, you hand over the thurible and then take the boat back.

When you incense people, face them. Smile. Bow to them. They will bow to you. Then swing the thurible to send up clouds of smoke. Depending on what kind of thurible you use, your leader will show you how (and how many times) to swing it. Usually the presider will incense things like the cross or the altar or a holy image.

You may need to add more coal to the thurible before bringing it out at the preparation of the gifts. The coals that you put in before Mass began may have burned out by then. If the old coal is still glowing, you can simply add a new coal and blow a little bit to make the new one spark. If the first coals are burned out, you will have to light the new one with matches. But do this quickly and quietly so that no one knows you are doing it.

Don't cough or make funny faces when you are the thurifer. The holy smoke is an important part of our prayer. It may smell strange to you at first, but you'll get used to it. Remember the words of Psalm 141 whenever you are the thurifer: "My prayers rise like incense."

Prayers

A good prayer for servers to pray always is Psalm 100, found in the beginning of this book. Here are some other good prayers to learn and to pray. You might want to copy these prayers onto cards to carry in your pocket or put up in your room. Memorize the ones you use most of the time. Ask your mom or dad or leader to explain any words that you don't know.

Before Leaving for Church

This is from Psalm 122. Say it before you leave home to go to church to serve.

> I was glad when they said to me,
> "Let us go to the house of the LORD!"

Write your own prayer to say before leaving home to go to church to serve:

....

....

....

Before Serving Mass

Here are some prayers to say before serving Mass.

From Psalm 43:

> I will go to the altar of God,
>   to God my exceeding joy;
> and I will praise you . . . .

Another prayer:

> Thank you, God,
> for calling me to serve at your altar this day.
> Help me to be calm and joyful
>   to remember everything
>   and do my tasks well.
> I ask this in Jesus' name. Amen.

Write your own prayer to say before serving Mass:

....

....

....

Say this prayer from Psalm 92 before serving Morning and Evening Prayer.

> It is good to give thanks to the LORD,
>   to sing praises to your name, O Most High;
> to declare your steadfast love in the morning,
>   and your faithfulness by night,
> to the music of the lute and the harp,
>   to the melody of the lyre.

Say this prayer before serving a wedding.

> Holy God,
> Jesus went to a wedding
> and rejoiced with the bride and groom.
> Help me to bring joy to this wedding day
> by serving at your altar.
> I ask this in Jesus' name. Amen.

Say this prayer after serving a wedding.

> Holy God,
> Jesus went to a wedding
> and turned water into wine
> in the couple's time of need.
> Bless the couple
> whose wedding I helped with today.
> Bring them joy and peace together
> and be with them in their times of need. Amen.

Write your own prayer to say before or after serving a wedding:

....

....

....

Before and After Serving a Funeral

Say this prayer before serving a funeral.

> Living God,
> it is sad when someone dies.
> Jesus cried when his friend Lazarus died.
> And Mary wept when she held Jesus in her arms
>   after he died on the cross.
> You know our sadness, God.
> Help me to help others today
> by serving this funeral.
> And be with all of us when we are sad.
> I ask this in Jesus' name. Amen.

Write your own prayer to say before or after serving a funeral:

....

....

....

....

After Serving Daily Mass or Morning and Evening Prayer

Say this prayer from Psalm 27 after you serve Mass or Morning and Evening Prayer.

> One thing I asked of the LORD,
>   that will I seek after;
> to live in the house of the LORD
>   all the days of my life,
> to behold the beauty of the LORD,
>   and to inquire in his temple.

Write your own prayer to say after serving Mass or Morning and Evening Prayer:

....

....

....

....

Say this prayer if you don't feel like serving when you are scheduled to serve.

> God,
> you always take care of us
> and you always do what you promise.
> I promised to serve today,
> but I don't feel like going.
> Help me to do what I promised,
> to serve you by serving in the church.
> I ask this in the name of Jesus. Amen.

Write your own prayer to say when you don't feel like serving:

....

....

....

....

Glory to God

We use this prayer at Sunday Mass, but not during Advent or Lent. During Advent we don't sing it because we are saving it for Christmas: It is the song that the angels sang when Jesus was born! During Lent we don't sing it because we remember that the Israelites were so sad when they had to leave their country that they stopped singing. But other times we are glad to sing this prayer. You can use this prayer when you wake up or any time that you are happy.

> Glory to God in the highest,
> and on earth peace to people
>   of good will.
>
> We praise you,
> we bless you,
> we adore you,
> we glorify you,
> we give you thanks for your
>   great glory,
> Lord God, heavenly King,
> O God, almighty Father.
>
> Lord Jesus Christ, Only Begotten Son,
> Lord God, Lamb of God,
>   Son of the Father,
>
> you take away the sins of the world,
>   have mercy on us;
> you take away the sins of the world,
>   receive our prayer;
> you are seated at the right hand
>   of the Father,
>   have mercy on us.
>
> For you alone are the Holy One,
> you alone are the Lord,
> you alone are the Most High,
> Jesus Christ,
> with the Holy Spirit,
> in the glory of God the Father.
> Amen.

Alleluia!

This is a one-word prayer! It comes from the Hebrew word *hallelujah*. Some people say it means "Praise God." But it's hard to explain all that it means. Have you ever been so happy that you didn't know what to say? Well, that's what this most joyful prayer word is like. We don't sing this joyful prayer word during the season of Lent. Then we remember how sad the Israelites were when they were forced to leave their homes. But during Eastertime, we sing it all the time, and sometimes three times in a row. That's how happy we are at Easter!

Alleluia!

The Creed

In the creed we tell each other — and the whole world — what we believe about God. On Sundays we say the Nicene Creed (which you can find in *The Roman Missal*) and sometimes we use the Apostles' Creed (below).

I believe in God,
the Father almighty,
Creator of heaven and earth,
and in Jesus Christ, his only Son, our Lord,
who was conceived by the Holy Spirit,
born of the Virgin Mary,
suffered under Pontius Pilate,
was crucified, died and was buried;
he descended into hell;
on the third day he rose again from the dead;
he ascended into heaven,
and is seated at the right hand of God the Father almighty;
from there he will come to judge the living and the dead.

I believe in the Holy Spirit,
the holy catholic Church,
the communion of saints,
the forgiveness of sins,
the resurrection of the body,
and life everlasting. Amen.

Holy, Holy, Holy

We sing this prayer at the heart of the Mass, when we are giving thanks and praise over the bread and the wine. This prayer comes from the Bible. The first part is the song that Isaiah heard the angels singing before God's throne in the Temple. The second part is the song that the people of Jerusalem sang when Jesus came into the city on Palm Sunday, and it's from a psalm.

The word "Hosanna!" is like the word "Alleluia!" It's hard to explain all that it means. It's a shout of joy and of praise, like saying "Awesome!" You can use this prayer at any time, especially when you see or hear or feel something that reminds you of how great and wonderful God is.

Holy, Holy, Holy Lord God of hosts.
Heaven and earth are full of your glory.
Hosanna in the highest!
Blessed is he who comes in the name of the Lord.
Hosanna in the highest!

The Lord's Prayer

You probably know this version of the prayer that Jesus taught us:

Our Father,
who art in heaven,
hallowed be your Name.
Your kingdom come,
your will be done
on earth as it is in heaven.
Give us this day our daily bread;
and forgive us our trespasses
as we forgive those
    who trespass us against us.
Lead us not into temptation,
but deliver us from evil.
For the kingdom, the power
and the glory are yours,
now and forever. Amen.

Here's another way of praying Jesus' prayer that many Christian communities use:

Our Father in heaven,
hallowed be your name,
your kingdom come,
your will be done,
    on earth as in heaven.
Give us today our daily bread.
Forgive us our sins
    as we forgive those
    who sin against us.
Save us from the time of trial
    and deliver us from evil.
For the kingdom, the power
    and the glory are yours,
    now and forever. Amen.

Amen!

Like "Alleluia!" another one-word prayer is the Hebrew word *Amen*. It means "Yes, let it be so." Most often we use it at the end of another prayer, as the last word.

Amen!

Server's Glossary

acolyte: another name for server; a minister who helps the priest and deacon at the chair and at the altar.

alb: the holy robe of baptism that ministers wear at the liturgy.

altar: the holy table of the Lord.

ambo: the holy place where God's word is spoken.

ambry: the cabinet that holds the holy oils, usually near the font.

archbishop: a bishop who serves as leader of an archdiocese.

archdiocese: an especially large or important diocese.

aspergillum: the metal stick or the branch from a bush that is used to sprinkle holy water.

assembly: all of the baptized people and all the people preparing to be baptized, gathered together around Christ Jesus, gathered together to celebrate the liturgy. Another word for assembly is *congregation.* Other names for the assembly are "the people of God," "the Body of Christ" and "the church."

benediction: a Latin word that means "blessing"; a service with singing and scripture readings and prayers where we worship Jesus in the holy bread of the eucharist, and the presider blesses the assembly by holding the holy bread of the eucharist up high.

Benedictus: the Latin name of the song that Zechariah sang when the angel told him that he would be the father of John the Baptist, and that Jesus would come to save us all.

boat: the container that holds the grains of incense before they are burned. The boat has a spoon that goes with it.

bishop: the head priest and teacher and leader in the church.

cantor: a minister who leads the singing and sings the verses of the psalm.

cassock: the long black robe that priests and servers sometimes wear. More often, servers wear an alb.

cathedral: the bishop's church building.

chalice: a cup that holds the holy wine that becomes the blood of Christ.

chasuble: the large colored garment that the priest wears over the other vestments.

choir: ministers who lead the singing and sometimes sing songs to lead the prayer of the assembly.

chrism: the holy oil used to anoint people in baptism, confirmation and ordination. It is made from olive oil and a special perfume. In the Bible, chrism was used to anoint priests, prophets and rulers. The name "Christ" means "the Anointed One" of God. The chrism is kept in the ambry.

church: the people of God who are baptized (or preparing to be baptized); the members (the hands and feet, eyes and ears) of the body of Christ (and Christ is the head of the body). "Church" is our name, and we give our name to the building where we gather to do our most important work: We worship God in the church building.

ciborium: a vessel that holds the gift of bread that becomes the body of Christ.

cincture: a belt made of rope.

coffin: the long box that holds the body of a dead person.

communion minister: a minister who helps share the body and the blood of Christ in the assembly.

congregation: another word for assembly. It means "the people called together" by God.

corporal: a linen cloth that is put on the altar, over the altar cloth, under the gifts of bread and wine.

cope: a large cape worn by a minister on special occasions.

credence table: the small table that holds the cups and plates and napkins and book when they are not being used.

creed: a speech that all baptized people make to say what they believe about God. At Mass we say the Nicene Creed or the Apostles' Creed.

crossbearer: the minister who carries the cross in procession. Another name for crossbearer is crucifer.

crosier: the shepherd's staff that the bishop carries. The bishop reminds us of Jesus, the good shepherd who leads and cares for us.

crucifer: the minister who carries the cross in procession. Another name for crucifer is crossbearer.

cruet: a vessel that holds water or wine.

dalmatic: an outer robe worn by deacons. It is shaped like a shirt that is too big.

deacon: a minister ordained to serve the poor and to serve the assembly by giving directions, reading the gospel, preaching and assisting at the altar.

diocese: all the parish churches in a particular area. The pastor of the whole diocese is the bishop.

evangelary: the book that has the gospel readings in it.

Evening Prayer: the liturgy when the sun sets; we sing psalms and songs to thank God for the day and for the light of Christ that shines like a candle in the night, and to ask God to watch over us in the evening.

finger towel/hand towel: a linen napkin used to dry the presider's hands.

flagon: a large vessel that holds the wine.

font: the large vessel or pool of holy water used in baptism.

genuflect: a sign of love for God that we show when we go down on one bended knee.

gifts table: the table that holds the bread and the wine before it is presented at the altar.

Gloria: the Latin name for the song that the angels sang when Jesus was born, and the song that we sing at Mass: "Glory to God in the highest!"

gospel: a Greek word that means "good news." There are four gospels in the Bible; they are the books that tell about the life and work of Jesus.

holy oils: the oils used for anointing the sick, for anointing those to be baptized and the special perfumed oil called chrism used for anointing people at their baptism. The bishop consecrates lots and lots of holy oils for all the churches in the diocese, and the churches receive their new oils on Holy Thursday.

homily: the speech that the bishop, priest or deacon gives after the scripture readings. The homily helps us understand what we have just heard from the Bible. It helps us to think about how we can live closer to God by helping others. And it makes us ready to lift up our hearts to God in the eucharistic prayer of the Mass.

humeral veil: a short robe that the presider wears around the shoulders to hold a vessel with the holy bread of the eucharist, or another minister wears to hold other things. It is used during devotions, but not at Mass.

icon: a holy picture of Jesus, Mary, a saint or an angel.

lavabo bowl: the bowl to use to wash the presider's hand. The word *lavabo* is Latin and it means "I wash."

lectionary: the book of the scripture readings. Each reading is called a "lection" or "lesson."

lector: a minister who reads the scripture readings.

liturgy: a Greek word that means "work of the people." It is the name that we give to our celebrations of the eucharist, of baptism and confirmation, of penance and the anointing of the sick, of marriage and ordination, of Morning and Evening Prayer.

lunette: a small glass container that holds the host and is put inside the monstrance.

Magnificat: the Latin name for the song that Mary sang when the angel told her that she would be Jesus' mother. It means "I praise God." The church sings Mary's song at Evening Prayer.

miter: the bishop's tall pointy hat.

monstrance: a large vessel used to show people the holy bread that is the body of Christ.

Morning Prayer: the liturgy in the morning when we sing psalms and songs to give God thanks for the rising sun and to ask God's help in the day to come.

music minister: the minister who organizes the music for the liturgy. Sometimes the music minister plays the organ, piano, guitar or other instrument, directs the choir and is the leader of the cantors.

pall: a large cloth draped over the coffin like an alb, to remind us that the person who has died is baptized.

pastor: the priest who takes care of a particular parish.

paten: a plate that holds the gift of bread that becomes the body of Christ.

presider: the minister who leads the assembly at liturgy. At Mass, the presider is a priest. The deacon or another baptized person may be the presider at weddings, funerals or baptisms, Morning Prayer, Evening Prayer or devotions.

priest: a minister ordained to serve in a special way as a leader of the assembly, to proclaim the gospel and to celebrate the sacraments.

pope: the bishop of Rome, who serves as pastor of the whole church.

procession: a parade, when baptized people walk and sing together.

psalm: a holy song from the Bible. The psalms were the hymns that Jesus and his first followers would have sung when they prayed to God. Now the church sings the psalms at Morning Prayer, at Evening Prayer, at Mass (after the first reading) and at other times, too.

purificator: a linen napkin used to wipe the cup that holds the blood of Christ.

pyx: a small vessel to hold the holy bread of the eucharist when a minister carries it out of church to people who are sick.

Roman Missal: the book of the prayers for Mass.

sacristan: a minister who takes care of all the things in the sacristy, and who helps prepare all the things needed for liturgy.

sacristy: the room in which all the things used in the liturgy are stored and cared for and prepared.

sanctuary: the space around the altar and ambo. The word comes from a Latin word and means "holy place."

Sanctus: the Latin name for the song that the angels sing around God's throne, and the song that we sing at Mass that starts "Holy, holy, holy." The Latin word *sanctus* means "holy."

server: a minister who helps the priest and the deacon at the chair and at the altar. Another name for server is acolyte. Servers can be adults, teenagers or kids. The pope says that both boys and girls can be servers.

stole: the long vestment worn around the neck by a priest or deacon.

surplice: a short white garment worn over the cassock at liturgy. The surplice is like an alb that is too short. Some surplices have fancy trimmings on them, and some don't.

tabernacle: the large vessel that holds the vessel of the holy bread of the eucharist, the body of Christ.

thurible: the pot that holds the charcoal on which incense is burned. The thurible can be a metal pot on a chain, or it may be a glass or ceramic pot filled with sand or stones.

thurifer: a minister who carries the incense pot (called a thurible).

usher: a minister who helps welcome people, seat people, direct processions and collect the gifts of money for the church and for the poor.

zucchetto: the bishop's small red cap.